符号中国 SIGNS OF CHINA

秦砖汉瓦

QIN BRICKS AND HAN TILES

"符号中国"编写组 ◎ 编著

中央民族大学出版社
China Minzu University Press

图书在版编目(CIP)数据

秦砖汉瓦：汉文、英文/"符号中国"编写组编著. —北京：中央民族大学出版社，2024.9
（符号中国）
ISBN 978-7-5660-2320-9

Ⅰ.①秦… Ⅱ.①符… Ⅲ.①古砖—介绍—中国—秦汉时代—汉、英②古瓦—介绍—中国—秦汉时代—汉、英 Ⅳ.①K876.3

中国国家版本馆CIP数据核字（2023）第255788号

符号中国：秦砖汉瓦 QIN BRICKS AND HAN TILES

编　　著	"符号中国"编写组
策划编辑	沙　平
责任编辑	杨爱新
英文编辑	邱　械
美术编辑	曹　娜　郑亚超　洪　涛
出版发行	中央民族大学出版社
	北京市海淀区中关村南大街27号　邮编：100081
	电话：（010）68472815（发行部）　传真：（010）68933757（发行部）
	（010）68932218（总编室）　　　　（010）68932447（办公室）
经 销 者	全国各地新华书店
印 刷 厂	北京兴星伟业印刷有限公司
开　　本	787 mm×1092 mm　1/16　印张：9
字　　数	124千字
版　　次	2024年9月第1版　2024年9月第1次印刷
书　　号	ISBN 978-7-5660-2320-9
定　　价	58.00元

版权所有　侵权必究

"符号中国"丛书编委会

唐兰东　巴哈提　杨国华　孟靖朝　赵秀琴

本册编写者

王亦儒

前言 Preface

秦砖汉瓦并非是指秦朝的砖、汉代的瓦，而是后世为纪念和说明秦汉时期建筑装饰的辉煌和鼎盛，对这一时期砖瓦的统称，现在也通常用来形容带有中国传统文化风格的古建筑。

两千多年前的秦、汉两朝对中国历史有着深远的影响，这一时期的砖和瓦虽然只是建筑的普通构件，但一直受到后世学者和艺术家的青睐，成为学术研究和艺术品鉴、收藏的一个文化门类。

秦砖汉瓦是秦汉文化的重要组成部

The term "Qin bricks and Han tiles" doesn't refer to the bricks of the Qin Dynasty or the tiles of the Han Dynasty, but rather a term that collectively refers to the bricks and tiles of these periods and is used by people in later generations to commemorate and illustrate the brilliance and prosperity of architectural decoration art during the Qin and Han dynasties (221 B.C.-220A.D.). It is now commonly used to describe ancient architecture with traditional Chinese cultural style.

The Qin and Han dynasties, over 2,000 years ago, had a far-reaching effect on Chinese history. Although the bricks and tiles from these periods were merely ordinary components of architecture, they have constituted a cultural category of academic and artistic research favored by scholars and artists throughout later ages.

Qin bricks and Han tiles are important cultural parts of the Qin and Han dynasties and parts of the time-honored and profound traditional Chinese cultural. Through fine characters and gorgeous patterns, they represented the history of the Qin and Han

分，也是中华民族悠久、博大的传统文化的组成部分。它们以精美的文字、华丽的图案再现了秦汉帝国的历史，在考古、历史、美术和书法艺术以及思想文化研究中，都具有极高的价值。秦砖汉瓦与甲骨文、青铜器、彩陶、简牍、玺印、封泥同享盛誉，是中华文明中一颗璀璨的明珠，是中国古代灿烂文化的重要组成部分。

本书全方位地展现了秦砖汉瓦的历史文化价值和艺术成就，还收集了众多图片，以供读者更全面、直观地感受中国秦砖汉瓦的魅力。

empires, being of high value in research on archeology, history, art, calligraphy, ideology and culture. As a shining pearl of Chinese civilization, Qin bricks and Han tiles share a high reputation with the oracle bone inscriptions, bronze ware, painted potters bamboo slips, imperial seals and sealing clay and became a crucial part of the splendid culture of ancient China.

This book fully demonstrates the historical and cultural values, as well as the artistic achievements of Qin bricks and Han tiles. Meanwhile, an ample collection of pictures is also available for readers to obtain a more comprehensive and intuitive experience of the charm of Chinese Qin bricks and Han tiles.

目录 Contents

秦砖汉瓦概述
Overview of Qin Bricks and Han Tiles 001

秦砖与汉瓦的起源
Origin of Qin Bricks and Han Tiles 002

秦砖与汉瓦
Qin Bricks and Han Tiles 015

砖
Bricks 041

素面砖
Plain-surface Bricks 042

花纹砖
Patterned Bricks 045

铭文砖
Inscription-patterned Bricks 050

画像砖
Portrayal Bricks 055

瓦当
Eaves Tiles 089

素面瓦当
Plain-surface Eaves Tiles 093

图案瓦当
Patterned Eaves Tiles 095

文字瓦当
Inscription-patterned Eaves Tiles 114

秦砖汉瓦概述
Overview of Qin Bricks and Han Tiles

　　秦、汉两朝是中国历史上的强盛时期，而秦砖汉瓦是这一历史时期鲜明的文化符号，它们真实再现了悠久古老、博大精深、源远流长的中华文明，将中国古代社会生活真实地反映出来。这里的一砖就是一页鲜活的历史，这里的一瓦就是一个耐人寻味的故事。

The Qin and Han dynasties were powerful and prosperous periods in ancient China, and Qin bricks and Han tiles were distinctive cultural symbols of these historical periods. They vividly relive the vast, profound and long history of Chinese civilization and reflect the social life of ancient China. Here, each brick is a page of living history, and each tile contains an intriguing story.

> 秦砖与汉瓦的起源

砖和瓦是重要的建筑材料，它们的出现标志着中国古代建筑的巨大进步。砖瓦属于建筑陶器，中国陶器的烧制和使用有超过万年的悠久历史。陶器出现后，砖瓦也被发明出来，并且得到了广泛的使用，古文献中就有对夏商时期砖瓦使用的记载。砖瓦的最早实物见于仰韶文化（前5000—前3000）遗址。

砖最早用来铺地和砌壁面，后来用于筑墙等。最早的砖是由土坯烧制而成的。1973年考古工作者对河北商代中晚期文化遗址进行发掘时，发现房址14座，其中最大的6座房址都以木柱为房架，墙壁以夯土和土坯砌筑。这种土坯就是砖的萌芽。后来，人们受制陶技术的启发，将土坯入窑烧制，其硬度大大提高，这就是砖。

> Origin of Qin Bricks and Han Tiles

Bricks and tiles are important building materials. Their emergence in history marked a great progress in ancient Chinese architecture. Bricks and tiles are earthenware used for construction. The firing and use of Chinese ceramics have a history spanning over ten thousand years. After the appearance of pottery, bricks and tiles were also invented and put into use widely. Ancient literature has documented the use of bricks and tiles during the Xia and Shang dynasties (approx. 2070 B.C.-1046 B.C.). The earliest bricks and tiles were found in Yangshao Culture (approx. 5000 B.C.-3000 B.C.) Relic Site.

The earliest bricks were used to pave floors and later to construct walls. The earliest bricks were made from adobe. In 1973, when excavating the cultural relics of the mid-late Shang Dynasty in Hebei Province, archaeologists discovered 14

1976年，在陕西扶风的周原遗址上，考古人员发现了先周时期的空心砖、条砖和板瓦。周原遗址是周文化的发祥地和灭商之前周人的聚居地，也是周人祭祀天地、祖先和神祇的地方。大量出土的砖瓦显示出这个遗址曾有过类似宫殿的高大建筑。这些砖瓦的发现将中国使用砖瓦的历史提前了八百多年。

- 陶罐（新石器时代）
陶器作为一种器具，在生活中应用于盛放食物、汲水、煮水和储物等。
Ceramic Pot (the Neolithic Age, approximately 8,000 years ago)
Ceramic ware was used in everyday life as eating utensils, storage ware and so on.

housing sites, among which the largest one contained six rooms, all framed with wood poles. And their walls were built of rammed mud and adobe. This kind of adobe was the origin of bricks. Later, inspired by pottery making, people began to put adobe into the kiln and fired it into bricks that were consequently harder. This was the birth of bricks.

In 1976, archaeologists discovered hollow bricks, bar bricks and pan tiles dating back to the early Zhou period at the Zhouyuan ruins in Fufeng, Shaanxi Province. The ruins of Zhouyuan was the birthplace of Zhou culture and the settlement of the Zhou people before they defeated the Shang Dynasty (1600 B.C. -1046 B.C.). It was also a sacred site where Zhou people worshiped heaven and earth, their ancestors and gods. A large number of bricks and tiles excavated at the ruins showed that tall architecture such as palace once towered there. The discovery of these bricks and tiles brings the dates for the use of bricks and tiles in Chinese history earlier by 800 years.

In 2006, when archaeologists were excavating a group of large buildings at the Zhouyuan ruins, they unearthed a brick 1 m long, 30 cm wide and 5 cm

• 弦纹斜线纹半瓦当（西周）
Semi-cylindrical Eaves Tile with Patterns of String Lines and Oblique Lines (Western Zhou Dynasty, 1046 B.C.-771 B.C.)

2006年，考古人员同样是在周原遗址对一组大型建筑遗址进行发掘时，挖出了一块长达1米、宽30厘米、厚5厘米的板砖，砖体呈灰褐色，上面有密密麻麻的绳纹。这块巨大的板砖被称为"西周第一板砖"。

瓦当就是陶制筒瓦顶端下垂的特定部分，即瓦的头端，俗称"瓦头"。其独特的造型便于屋顶排水，主要起着保护屋檐、防止风雨侵蚀、延长建筑物寿命的作用。

根据考古资料，迄今为止中国发现最早的瓦当是陕西周原凤雏遗址出土的西周晚期的半圆形瓦当。西周时期的瓦当主要有素面瓦当和饰有纹样的图案瓦当两种，素面瓦

thick. The brick was taupe in color with dense patterns of cords across its surfaces. This large brick was known as the First Pan Brick of the Western Zhou Dynasty.

Eaves tiles are the overhanging part of the earthen tile, that is, the top end of an eaves tile, commonly known as the tile head. The unique shape of eaves tiles facilitates the flow of water over the roof and plays a major role in protecting eaves, preventing erosion from wind and rain and prolonging the life of the building.

According to archaeological data, the earliest eaves tiles discovered in China to date were excavated from the Fengchu ruins of the late-period of the Western Zhou Dynasty in Zhouyuan, Shaanxi Province. These eaves tiles come in two major types, the plain-surface eaves tiles and the patterned eaves tiles. Plain-surface eaves tiles are either semi-circular or circular in shape while the patterned eaves tiles are rich in decorations of double-ring patterns, cord patterns, animal patterns, vegetation patterrs, cloud patterns, etc. Eaves tiles with patterns of double rings and cords are generally semi-circular in shape while eaves tiles with other patterns are mostly circular and possess a certain degree of formal beauty.

弄瓦之喜

在两千多年前的诗歌总集《诗经》中，有一首祝贺贵族新建宫室落成的颂诗："乃生男子，载寝之床，载衣之裳，载弄之璋。其泣喤喤，朱芾斯皇，室家君王。乃生女子，载寝之地，载衣之裼，载弄之瓦。无非无仪，唯酒食是议，无父母诒罹。"这首诗歌翻译成现代汉语是这样的：在这栋新的宫室里，如果生下男孩，要给他玉璋（玉器的一种，多见于战国以前，是天子祭祀山川的器物）当玩具，将来他一定有出息，地位尊贵，会成为王侯；如果生下女孩，就给她瓦（此处瓦指陶制纺锤，即梭子）当玩具，这女孩长大后定会是个既精通女工、又明事理的持家能手。后来，人们借用这种贺词，把生男孩称做"弄璋之喜"，生女孩称做"弄瓦之喜"。在现代人看来，璋为玉质，瓦为陶制，两者质地截然不同，弄璋、弄瓦有着明显的褒贬之分和性别歧视意味。其实，陶制砖瓦本身的材质虽然无法和玉相比，但在中国古代，制作精良、纹饰美观的砖瓦大多是皇家贵族、世家大族的专用品，同样价格不菲。

- 精美的陶制砖雕
  Exquisite Ceramic Brick Carving

Joy of Playing with Tiles

In the poetry collection *The Book of Songs* compiled 2,000 year ago, there's a poem in an ode form to celebrate the completion of a new palace for an aristocrat. When translated into modern Chinese, it reads: In this newly-built palace, if a boy is born, he will be given a jade tablet (a type of jade commonly seen prior to the Warring States Period, 475 B.C.-221 B.C., and used by emperors to worship the mountains and rivers) as a toy so that he will excel in the future, obtain a high position and eventually become a nobleman. If a girl is born, she will be given a tile (tile referred to a ceramic spindle at that time) as a toy so that she will grow up to be skilled in needlework and become a housekeeping expert with clear wit. Later, based on this allusion, the birth of a baby boy is called the "joy of playing with tablets" and the coming of a baby girl, the "joy of playing with tiles". In the minds of modern people, a jade tablet and a tile differ obviously in quality and the "joy of playing with tablets" and "joy of playing with tiles" may suggest gender discrimination. Although the earthen material used to make bricks and tiles cannot rival jade, well-made and beautifully-patterned bricks and tiles were actually special items exclusively used by noblemen and aristocratic families in ancient China, and were valuable as well.

当有半圆形和圆形，图案瓦当纹样特别丰富，有重环纹、绳纹、动物纹、植物纹、云纹等。重环纹和绳纹瓦当一般为半圆形，其他纹饰的

The Warring States Period (475 B.C.-221 B.C.) was a time that witnessed significant changes in Chinese history. The production techniques of bricks and tiles made considerable progress during this period. Since eaves tiles were already pervasive in a lot of palace architecture in

• 绳纹陶水管（春秋）
中国最早的建筑陶器是新石器时期就已出现的陶水管。
Cord-patterned Ceramic Water Pipe (Spring and Autumn Period, 770 B.C.-476 B.C.)
The earliest Chinese ceramic ware used in architecture was the ceramic water pipe in the Neolithic Age.

• 秦画像故事瓦当（战国）

此瓦当表现了两千多年前秦国先民理想中的人与动物、人与自然和谐共处的美好画面。

Eaves Tile with Portrait Tales from Qin (Warring States Period, 475 B.C.-221 B.C.)

This eaves tile illustrates the ideal scene of harmonious coexistence between man and animals and between man and nature as desired by the ancient people of Qin more than 2,000 years ago.

瓦当以圆形的居多，已具备一定的形式美。

战国（前475—前221）是中国历史上产生重大变革的时代，砖瓦的生产工艺在这一时期取得了长足的进步。各诸侯国的宫室建筑已经较多地使用瓦当，瓦当的造型和图案题材都出现了质的飞跃，并呈现出鲜明的地域特色。其中，以齐国都城（今山东淄博）的树木双兽纹半圆瓦当、燕国下都（今河北易县）的饕餮纹半圆瓦当、秦故都雍城（今陕西凤翔）的动物纹圆瓦当和咸阳的云纹葵纹瓦当为最佳，而瓦当文化的鼎盛时期是在秦汉。

feudal states, both the shapes and themes of patterns acquired great leaps with distinct regional characteristics. Among them, the best ones were the semi-circular eaves tiles with patterns of trees and paired animals from the capital of the Qi State (currently Zibo in Shandong Province), the semi-circular eaves tiles patterned with images of *Taotie* (a mythical ferocious monster) from the auxiliary capital (currently Yixian County in Hebei Province) of the Yan State, the animal-patterned circular eaves tiles from Yongcheng City, the old capital of the Qin State, and the eaves tiles with patterns of clouds and sunflowers from Xianyang, the capital of the Qin State. The culture of eaves tiles reached its heyday during the Qin and Han dynasties (221 B.C.-220 A.D.).

砖瓦的烧制

古时，砖瓦的烧制技术并不复杂，但经验很重要。首先将半成品的砖瓦，沿土窑的内壁整齐地摆放好，一般为瓦片在上，砖块在下。然后把30厘米长的硬木整齐地排放在砖和瓦的缝隙之中（硬木有助于保持燃烧火力）。做好这些后，就可以建窑门了。窑门要建成上下对称的两个，上门添柴，下门出灰。再选个日子请烧窑师傅点火，点火后是烧窑之人最为辛苦的时候，需要日夜添柴，不得休息。这时添的主要是毛柴，就是带叶子混有杂草的柴火，这有利于燃烧。过五天左右，要观察窑内的温度等情况。如果火候不到，没烧透，不牢固；火候过头，砖瓦变形，会前功尽弃。火候差不多时就可以闭窑，也就是把窑门用砖块封死，仅凭窑顶的小洞口提供氧气供窑内燃烧。烧制需要一定的时间，等窑内的温度降到可以启窑时，砖瓦的烧制工序就算完成了。检验砖瓦烧制得是否成功的方法，是用成品相互打击，如果发出的是清脆的金属声音，而又不变形，就算是烧成功了。

Firing of Bricks and Tiles

Although the firing techniques of bricks and tiles were not complicated in ancient times, experience counted a lot. First, the half-finished bricks and tiles were placed neatly along the internal wall of the clay kiln where the tiles were usually placed on top of the bricks. Then, pieces of 30-cm-long hard wood were inserted vertically in the space between the

• 古砖瓦窑遗址 （图片提供：FOTOE）

中国古代的砖瓦一般都在砖瓦窑烧制。这种用来烧制砖瓦的窑洞由多个洞口和一个出烟的烟囱组成，用木头或煤屑做燃料，温度极高，可达上千度。

Ruins of Ancient Brick Kiln

Ancient Chinese bricks and tiles were generally fired in kilns. The kiln to fire the bricks and tiles comprised multiples holes and a chimney to let out smoke. Wood and coal dust were generally used as fuel and the resulting temperature could go up to 1,000 degrees Celsius.

• 琉璃瓦
Glazed Tiles

bricks and tiles (hard wood helps maintain the heat). After this, the kiln door can be built. The kiln door should be established symmetrically in two parts horizontally. Wood was added through the upper opening and ashes were raked out from the lower one. Then, a firing master was invited to light the fire on a chosen auspicious date. The work involved after the ignition was the most toilsome for firing workers since it needed constant wood replenishment day and night. The fuel materials added at this time were basically crude wood, a mixture of leaves, weeds and firewood, which was conducive for burning. The temperature inside the kiln and other conditions were observed after approximately five days. If the heat was insufficient, the bricks and tiles would not be thoroughly baked and would lack hardness. If the heat was more than sufficient, the bricks and tiles would deform and bring all the previous efforts to nothing. When the heat is appropriate, the kiln could be closed. In other words, the kiln door would be sealed with bricks, and only a small hole left at the top of the kiln would provide oxygen for the fire inside. The firing required a specific amount of time. Once the temperature inside the kiln dropped to the point where the kiln was ready to be opened, the firing process was finished. The finished bricks and tiles were knocked against each other to test whether the firing process was successful. If they gave out crisp sounds without being deformed, the firing was then considered successful.

• 板瓦（西周）

西周的板瓦上多带有瓦钉和瓦环，主要是为了防止瓦件下滑和固定筒瓦。

Pan Tile (Western Zhou Dynasty, 1046 B.C.-771 B.C.)

Pan tiles from the Western Zhou Dynasty (1046B.C.-771 B.C.) generally have tile buttons and tile rings to prevent the tiles from sliding and to fasten the cylindrical tiles.

• 绳纹筒瓦

绳纹是陶器的装饰纹样之一，是新石器时代至商周时期陶器上最常见的纹饰。其制作方法是在陶坯（陶器的生坯）制好后，待半干时，用缠有绳子的陶拍在陶坯上拍印，留下绳纹，再入窑焙烧。

Cord-patterned Cylindrical Tiles

The pattern of cords is one of the decorative patterns for ceramic ware. It was the pattern most commonly used on ceramics from the Neolithic Age (approx. 8,000 years ago) to the Shang and Zhou dynasties (1600B.C.-221 B.C.). To produce a cord pattern, a piece of greenware (the green body of the ceramic ware) is made and half-dried, then a ceramic bat wrapped with a rope is pressed on the greenware in order to leave the rope marks on it. The greenware with the imprints is then put into the kiln for firing.

• 土坯（图片提供：全景正片）

土坯是将黏土（一般为黄土）装在木板制成的模具（一般为50cm×25cm，厚度为10cm）中，用特制的石块或木板拍实，在开阔的阳光充足的地方晾晒干。一般用于砌墙建房，中国北方较常见。

Adobe

Adobe is a type of clay (generally loess) placed within wood molds (typically 50 cm by 25 cm with a thickness of 10 cm) and patted solid by a special stone tab or wooden plate before being left in a sunny and wide place to dry. Adobe is typically used to build walls or houses and more commonly seen in northern China.

- **灵寿古城建筑构件（战国）**

  在中国传统的房屋建筑中，房顶铺设有板瓦和筒瓦，在屋檐处安置瓦当。瓦当是最靠近屋檐的瓦的部件，瓦当后面就是筒瓦。

  Construction Components of Ancient Lingshou City (Warring States Period, 475 B.C.-221 B.C.)

  In ancient Chinese houses, pan tiles and cylindrical tiles were paved on the roof with eaves tiles placed at the protruding part of the eaves. The eaves tile is the component closest to the eaves. It can be seen that eaves tiles are in the front and cylindrical tiles are positioned behind.

- **凤纹瓦当（战国）**

  凤是古代传说中的神鸟，常用来象征祥瑞。

  Phoenix-patterned Eaves Tiles (Warring States Period, 475 B.C.-221 B.C.)

  The phoenix is a holy bird in ancient Chinese legend, symbolizing auspicious.

- **齐树木抽象植物纹半瓦当（战国）**

  瓦当上树木的枝条有繁有简，有曲有直。总的来看，早期植物纹瓦当的树枝较少，多弯曲，后来以直枝树木纹居多，也有带叶树木纹。

  Semi-cylindrical Eaves Tile with Patterns of a Tree and Abstract Vegetation from the Qi State (Warring States Period, 475 B.C.-221 B.C.)

  The branches of the tree on the eaves tile vary in complexity and curvature. In general, early vegetation-patterned eaves tiles had fewer branches, mostly curved. Later, branches of the tree pattern were mostly straight with leafy trees also seen.

秦砖汉瓦概述 / Overview of Qin Bricks and Han Tiles

- 树木"S"形云纹半瓦当（战国 齐）

树木双兽纹半瓦当可能早在春秋时期就开始使用。树木纹为齐国瓦当最主要的纹饰，通常瓦当正面饰以树木，左右饰以走兽、禽鸟、人物、乳钉、曲线、三角等纹饰，变化极为丰富。

Semi-cylindrical Eaves Tile with Patterns of a Tree and S-shaped Cloud (Qi State of the Warring States Period, 475 B.C.-221 B.C.)

The semi-cylindrical eaves tile with patterns of a tree and paired animals may have been used as early as the Spring and Autumn Period (770B.C.-476 B.C.). As the main patterns on eaves tiles in the Qi State, the tree pattern usually decorated the front surface of the eaves tile with a tree and various images on both sides including animals, birds, personage, studs, curve lines or triangles.

- 树木双马纹半瓦当片（战国 齐）

半圆瓦当，中间有一树，树下系两马，昂首相对，极富生活气息。

Semi-cylindrical Eaves Tile with Patterns of a Tree and Two Horses (Qi State of the Warring States Period, 475 B.C.-221 B.C.)

The semi-cylindrical eaves tile has a picture of a tree in the middle and two horses tethered to the tree with heads held high, full of a lively atmosphere.

- 树木双骑半瓦当（战国 齐）

树木双骑纹在战国时期很流行，图案一般是被绳子系于树干上的双鹿或双马。

Semi-cylindrical Eaves Tile with Patterns of a Tree and Two Riding Horses (Qi State of the Warring States Period, 475 B.C.-221 B.C.)

The semi-cylindrical eaves tile with patterns of a tree and two riding horses was popular in the Warring States Period (475B.C.-221 B.C.). Usually, the pattern was two deer or two horses tied to the trunk of the tree with ropes.

• 燕国饕餮纹瓦当（战国）

饕餮是一种想象中的神兽，是中国古人融合了自然界各种猛兽的特征，同时加以自己的想象创造出来的。饕餮纹有的有躯干和兽足，有的仅有兽面，兽面巨大而夸张，装饰性很强，故也称"兽面纹"。

Taotie-patterned Eaves Tile of the Yan State (Warring States Period, 475 B.C.-221 B.C.)

Taotie is an imaginary divine animal ancient Chinese people created by mixing the key characteristics of various wild animals from the natural world, coupled with a tint of imagination. Some *Taotie* patterns, also called animal-face patterns, have body and legs of animals while others may only have the face of an animal, sizable and exaggerated with high decorativeness.

• 燕国饕餮纹半瓦当（战国）

战国时期燕国的瓦当。燕国故地主要在今河北北部、辽宁西部，北京和天津等地区，出土的瓦当基本上都是半瓦当，早期为素面，其他有兽面纹等。

Taotie-patterned Semi-cylindrical Eaves Tile of the Yan State (Warring States Period, 475 B.C.-221 B.C.)

This is an eaves tile from the Yan State during the Warring States Period (475B.C.-221 B.C.). The Yan State was located in the region covering today's western Liaoning Province, Beijing, Tianjin and northern Hebei Province. Most of the unearthed eaves tiles of the early age there are semi-cylindrical with plain surfaces. Some of them are decorated with animal-face patterns.

• 双龙双凤纹半瓦当（战国）

这件瓦当构思巧妙，在如此小的空间里刻画出双龙双凤，画面紧凑又不失大气。

Semi-cylindrical Eaves Tile with Patterns of Two Loongs and Two Phoenixes (Warring States Period, 475 B.C.-221 B.C.)

The ingeniousness of this eaves tile lies in overlapped pairs of loongs and phoenixes in such a small space. The layout is compact without losing a grand atmosphere.

• 虎獐鱼豺瓦当（战国）

在陕西凤翔秦故都雍城遗址，考古工作者发现了秦国雍城制陶作坊，出土了2000多件以动物图案为主的秦瓦当，上面大多有纹饰和文字，有很高的艺术和考古价值。在许多以动物为图案的圆形瓦当中，有鹿纹、獾纹、虎纹、鱼纹、斗兽纹等。这些动物形象是以当时狩猎中常见的动物为原型的，反映了先秦时期狩猎活动的兴盛。

Eaves Tile with Patterns of a Tiger, a River Deer, a Fish and a Jackal (Warring States Period, 475 B.C.-221 B.C.)

In the ruins of Yongcheng City, the old capital of Qin, currently known as Fengxiang, in Shaanxi Province, archaeologists discovered a pottery workshop from Yongcheng City of the Qin Dynasty with more than 2,000 pieces of animal-patterned eaves tiles from the Qin Dynasty unearthed. Most of these eaves tiles are decorated with patterns and characters and imbued with high artistic and archaeological value. Among the animal-patterned cylindrical eaves tiles, images of deer, badgers, tigers, fish and fighting animals can be seen. They are the common animals in hunting activities at that time and reflect the booming of hunting activities in the Qin Dynasty.

• 夔凤瓦当（战国）

该瓦当中夔凤曲颈弯曲，尾部高扬，躯身呈弧形，姿态舒展，飘然而立，是夔凤纹中的佳品。凤鸟纹瓦当出土数量较多，种类丰富，目前发现的有6种之多。这些瓦当上的凤鸟形态有相同之处，基本为曲颈、长翅、长冠，长尾分叉且上翘，长翅振起呈奔走或飞翔状。

Eaves Tile with Patterns of *Kui*-phoenix (Warring States Period, 475 B.C.-221 B.C.)

The *Kui*-phoenix depicted on this eaves tile with the neck curved, tail held high and body stretched, floating in the air with a soothing posture, is a rare masterpiece among all the eaves tiles with the pattern of a *Kui*-phoenix. Phoenix-patterned eaves tiles have been excavated in large quantities and in great varieties. There are currently six different kinds discovered so far, all of which feature a similar stance, such as the curved neck, long wings, long crown, long forked tail held high and the pose in such a position as if the phoenix was about to run or fly.

> 秦砖与汉瓦

　　秦汉时期是中国封建社会的开端，也是中国建立大一统国家的开始。公元前221年，秦始皇统一六国，结束了诸侯割据的混乱局面，建立了第一个中央集权制的封建王朝。到了汉代，社会安定，生产力

> Qin Bricks and Han Tiles

The Qin and Han dynasties (221 B.C.-220 A.D.) saw the initiation of China's feudal society and marked the beginning of the establishment of a unified dynasty in Chinese history. In 221 B.C., when the first emperor of Qin unified the Six States and ended the chaos in the country that had been divided by feudal princes, the first centralized feudal dynasty was established. When it came to the Han Dynasty (206 B.C.-220 A.D.), social stability and well-developed productivity prompted massive construction projects in various regions. Combined with rapid advancements in the handicraft industry,

- 秦始皇陵兵马俑坑中的秦砖
  Qin Bricks from the Terracotta Warriors and Horses Pit of the First Emperor of Qin's Mausoleum

- **秦始皇陵兵马俑坑铺地砖**

  秦代人修建俑坑时铺设的砖。在秦始皇陵兵马俑坑中，过洞和部分长廊均铺设青砖，砖的规格有多种，仅一号坑内铺地砖就有4种：大型条砖（42厘米×19.5厘米×9.5厘米）、窄长条砖（41.5厘米×14厘米×9.5厘米）、小型条砖（28厘米×14厘米×7厘米）、近似方形大砖（23厘米×19.5厘米×9.5厘米）。其中小型条砖的数量最多。

Floor Bricks from Terracotta Warriors and Horses Pit in the First Emperor of Qin's Mausoleum

This is the brick used by the people of the Qin Dynasty to pave the floor of the terracotta pit. Inside the Terracotta Warrior and Horses Pit of the First Emperor of Qin's Mausoleum, the passage openings and corridors are paved with black bricks in varied specifications. The NO.1 pit alone is paved with four different types of bricks: large bar bricks (42 cm × 19.5 cm× 9.5 cm), narrow and long bar bricks (41.5 cm× 14 cm× 9.5 cm), small bar bricks (28 cm× 14 cm× 7 cm) and near-rectangular large brick (23 cm× 19.5 cm× 9.5 cm). Among them, the small bar bricks are the most common.

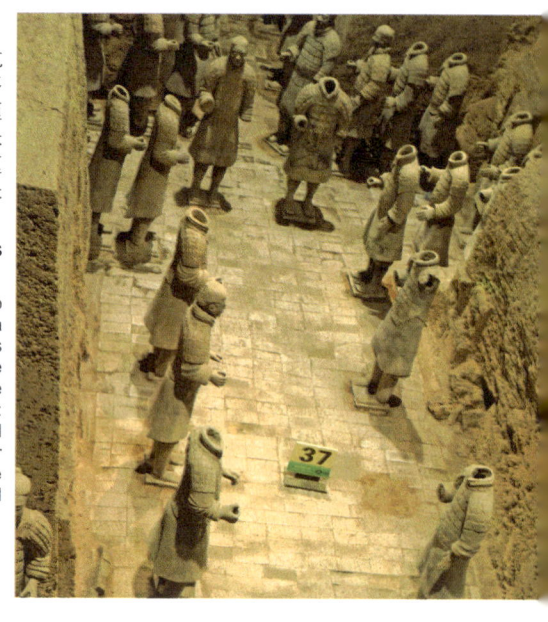

有了长足发展，各地都大兴土木，手工业突飞猛进，建筑业也得到了空前的发展。砖石结构的建筑在建构方法、式样和造型特征上都已形成体系并有了长足的发展，而砖瓦则在宫殿、陵墓、城防、水利工程以及民用住宅上发挥了重要作用。这一时期制陶业的生产规模、烧造技术，陶器的数量和质量都超过了以往，特别是富有特色的画像砖和各种纹饰的瓦当更被赋予极其重要的文化特征。

　　秦朝之前，砖大都用在宫殿、

the construction industry experienced unprecedented development. Buildings with masonry structures also made striding progress and developed systematic constructional methods and characteristics of styles and shapes. Meanwhile, bricks and tiles played a significant role in the construction of palaces, tombs, city defenses, water conservancies and civilian houses. The ceramic industry also made great progress in its production scale, firing technology and the product quantity and quality. Especially those portrayal bricks with distinctive features and patterned tiles with various decorations

秦始皇

　　秦始皇，姓嬴，名政，是中国历史上第一个大一统王朝秦朝的开国皇帝。公元前247年，13岁的嬴政继承王位，22岁时开始亲理朝政。自公元前230年到公元前221年，秦王嬴政先后灭韩、赵、魏、楚、燕、齐六国，完成统一大业，建立了一个中央集权的强大国家——秦朝。秦始皇统一六国后，又开疆拓土，奠定了今日中国的基本版图。他确立的一系列制度，开创了中国政治制度的基本模式。秦始皇认为自己的功劳胜过之前的"三皇五帝"，改称"皇帝"，他也是中国历史上第一个使用"皇帝"称号的君主，自称"始皇帝"。

The First Emperor of Qin

The First Emperor of Qin, Ying Zheng, is the founding emperor of the Qin Dynasty, the first unified dynasty in Chinese history. Ying Zheng inherited the throne at the age of 13 in 247 B.C. He began managing state affairs in person at the age of 22. From 230 B.C. to 221 B.C., the Six States of Han, Zhao, Wei, Chu, Yan and Qi were conquered successively and the great cause of national unification was accomplished with the Qin Dynasty; a powerful centralized state was established. After the First Emperor of Qin unified the Six States, he expanded his territory and laid down the basic domain of today's China. He also set up a series of systems, creating the basic patterns of the Chinese political system. The First Emperor of Qin believed that his contribution surpassed that of the "Three Sovereigns and Five Emperors". Therefore, he changed his title to emperor (meaning the heavenly governor) , making him the first monarch in Chinese history to use the title of emperor. He claimed himself to be the very first emperor.

墓葬等方面，砖上的花纹也多具有装饰性，并没有大规模应用在其他建筑上。秦汉之时，砖的使用多起来，不仅大量用于建筑装饰，而且开始具有承重作用，如构建城池、建造房屋等。

秦砖最早发现于陕西扶风云塘的灰坑之中，早期称为"秦方砖"。这种砖又厚又重，没有规

- **秦陵出土的秦砖**

  秦陵出土的砖都做工规矩，质地坚硬。据有关科研单位测定，这种秦砖的抗压能力是其他砖的两倍。在秦陵兵马俑一号坑的东南角还有一段砖墙，高165厘米，宽85厘米，砖系平铺叠筑，用细泥涂抹。这堵砖墙用于修补坍塌的土坑夯土边墙，是中国目前已知最早的砖墙。

A Qin Brick Unearthed from Qin's Mausoleum

Bricks excavated from the mausoleum are all made in a standardized size and have a hard texture. According to the measurement by a scientific research unit, the load-bearing capacity of this type of Qin brick is two times that of other bricks. There is also a section of brick wall located at the southeast corner of NO.1 pit, 165 cm in height and 85 cm in width. It is built with horizontally laid bricks piled up and daubed with fine mud. Although this brick wall was used to repair the collapsed sidewall of the pit, it is currently the oldest brick wall known in China.

were bestowed with extremely significant cultural characteristics.

Prior to the Qin Dynasty (221 B.C.-206 B.C.), bricks were generally used in palaces and tombs without large-scale application elsewhere and the patterns on bricks were decorative. During the Qin and Han dynasties, the application of bricks was increased. They were not only widely used as building decorations, but also shifted to a load-bearing role in fortresses and houses.

The earliest Qin bricks were discovered in an ash pit in Yuntang, Fufeng, Shaanxi Province. They were called the "rectangular bricks of Qin" early on. This type of brick was thick and heavy with no regular specifications and enough load-bearing capacity. After constant improvements, the rectangular bricks of Qin eventually became an important building material and were used in many important projects during the Qin Dynasty, such as the construction of palaces, city walls and tombs. They were made of Lishan soil, which is rich in minerals and became solid, durable and weighty after being processed. This kind of brick was also called the "lead brick".

Black bricks were most widely used for construction during the Qin Dynasty.

格，也没有足够的承重能力。后来经过不断的改进，秦方砖成为重要建材，广泛运用于秦代的许多重要工程，如宫殿、城墙、陵墓等。建筑所用之砖，在制造时多取用富含多种矿物质成分的骊山泥土作为原料，加工后，不仅非常坚固耐用，而且分量很重，此类秦砖又有"铅砖"之称。

秦代建筑用砖以青砖为主，在高山峻岭顶端筑起的万里长城，就是用这种青砖建造的伟大工程之一。长城用砖之多，举世罕见。

制砖业在汉代取得了长足的进步。西汉前期的砖多为小型砖。这种砖的特点是实心，呈长方形或正方形，装饰图案以几何纹为主。由于经过烧制的砖具有强度高、耐磨、耐水浸等特性，因此多用于建筑中的防水部位及易于磨损的部位。不但用在地面建筑上，也广泛用于地下墓葬中。为了增加砖在墓葬中的装饰性，还运用了雕刻技艺，这其中以画像砖最为著名。

瓦当的使用在秦汉时期也达到了高峰。从考古出土的瓦当看，秦汉时期的瓦当分布地域之广、纹饰之繁、制作之精，也都达到了前所

The Great Wall built on top of lofty mountains is one of the great projects involving such bricks. The number of bricks used in the Great Wall is huge even on a global scale.

Bricks experienced considerable progress in the Han Dynasty (206 B.C.-220 A.D.). Most of the bricks made in the early Western Han Dynasty (206 B.C.-25 A.D.) were small in size, solid in the core and generally rectangular or square in shape with geometric patterns. Since fired bricks are high in strength, abrasion-proof and water-resistant, they were mostly used on building parts that would otherwise be easily-worn and needed to be waterproof. In addition to overground construction, they were also used in underground tombs. To increase the decorativeness of bricks in tombs, sculpture craft was also applied. The most noted among them were portrayal bricks.

The use of eaves tiles reached its peak in the Qin and Han dynasties. According to archaeological findings in unearthed eaves tiles, the eaves tiles during this period had reached an unprecedented height in terms of distribution range, decoration complexity and product fineness. Plain-surface eaves tiles decreased in quantity during the Qin Dynasty and the early

万里长城

　　长城是古代中国在不同时期修筑的规模浩大的军事工程的统称。长城东西绵延上万公里，因此又称作"万里长城"。

　　早在春秋战国时期，各诸侯国为满足防御所需，就用城墙将烽火台连接起来，这就是最早的长城。秦始皇灭六国建立秦帝国后，公元前214年，派将军蒙恬率领30万人攻击匈奴，占据了河套地区，征集了几十万人修筑长城，并将之前各国修筑的旧长城连接起来，创造了人类建筑史上的奇迹。西汉继续对长城进行修建，先后修筑了近一万公里的长城，因此汉长城也是历史上最长的长城。此外，北朝、隋朝、明朝等都曾修筑过长城。现在看到的长城，以明朝修筑的最多。虽然万里长城早已失去了军事功能，但它作为中国古代人民创造的伟大奇迹，已成为中国的象征之一。

The Great Wall of China

The Great Wall is a general term referring to the large-scale military construction projects through different time periods in ancient China. The Great Wall, which stretches for 10,000 *Li* (a Chinese unit of length equal to 0.5 km) from east to west is therefore also called the Ten-thousands-*Li* Great Wall.

In the early Spring and Autumn Period (770 B.C.-476 B.C.), in order to meet the needs of defense, vassal states used to build city walls to link up beacon towers. This was the earliest form of the Great Wall. After the First Emperor of Qin conquered the Six States and

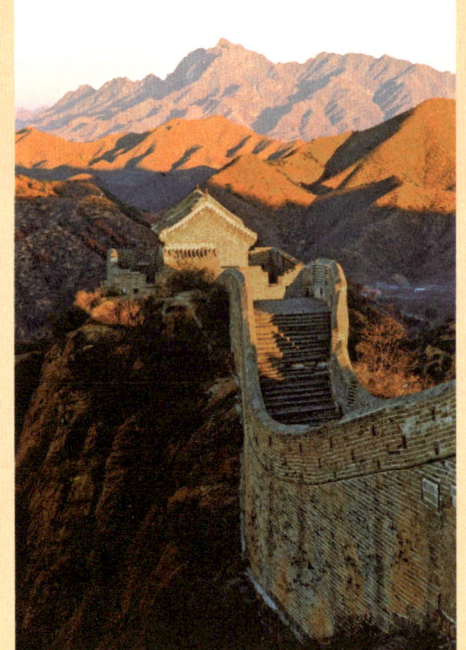

- 河北金山岭长城
  The Great Wall in Hebei Jinshanling

established the Qin Dynasty, he dispatched a troop of 300,000 soldiers led by general Meng Tian to attack the Huns and later conquered the Hetao region in 214 B.C. He then recruited hundreds of thousands of people to construct the Great Wall to link up the old city walls left by other states, which created a wonder in the history of human construction. In the Western Han Dynasty (206 B.C.-25 A.D.) the construction of the Great Wall was continued. The Han Dynasty built nearly 10,000 km of the Great Wall, making the Great Wall of Han the longest wall in history. Additionally, the Northern dynasties (386-581), the Sui Dynasty (581-618) and the Ming Dynasty (1368-1644) all built a great portion of the Great Wall. Most of the Great Wall we see today was built during the Ming Dynasty. The Great Wall has long lost its military function but, as a great wonder created by ancient Chinese people, it has become one of the symbols that stand for China.

- 万里长城
  The Great Wall of China

● 车马画像砖（汉）
Portrayal Brick of Chariots and Horses
(Han Dynasty, 206 B.C.-220 A.D.)

未有的高度。秦和西汉初期素面瓦当减少，多为图案瓦当，以圆瓦当为主，还有少量半圆瓦当和大半圆瓦当。秦代瓦当基本继承了战国晚期瓦当的样式，同时有所创新，云纹成为瓦当的主要纹饰，文字瓦当数量不多。西汉中晚期的素面瓦当数量极少，并逐渐消失，而以图案瓦当和文字瓦当为主，文字瓦当开始流行。瓦当图案种类极多，有麟凤、飞鸿、双鱼、玉兔、蟾蜍等数十种。与秦代的瓦当图案取材于现实生活不同，汉代的瓦当图像虽取材于现实，但又有高度的艺术夸

stage of the Western Han Dynasty (206 B.C.-25 A.D.), while patterned eaves tiles, mostly cylindrical ones, increased and a small part of them were semi-cylindrical ones and three-quarter cylindrical ones. Eaves tiles from the Qin Dynasty basically inherited the styles from the late Warring States Period (475 B.C.-221 B.C.) with some innovation. Cloud became the primary decoration pattern while inscription-patterned ones were not so common. During the mid-and-late Western Han Dynasty, the plain-surface eaves tiles decreased in number and eventually disappeared, while patterned and inscription-patterned ones became

• 人物画像砖（东汉）
Portrayal Brick of the People (Eastern Han Dynasty, 25-220)

• "四夷尽服"瓦当（汉）
Eaves Tile with Characters of *Siyi Jinfu* (Han Dynasty, 206 B.C.-220 A.D.)

• 蟾蜍玉兔瓦当拓片

此瓦当上的图案出自中国古代神话传说：嫦娥奔月。月宫中住着嫦娥、玉兔和蟾蜍，还有桂树。此瓦当将月宫盛况形象地展现出来：玉兔奔跑，蟾蜍出水，桂树环绕，美景尽显。

Eaves Tile with Patterns of Toad and Rabbit

The pattern of this eaves tile comes from the ancient Chinese mythology of Goddess Chang E's flight to the moon. Goddess Chang E lives in the moon palace along with the jade rabbit, the toad and laurel trees. This eaves tile vividly displays the prosperous scene at the moon palace: The jade rabbit is running; the toad is coming out of the water and the laurel trees surround the place with beautiful scenery.

张，想象力丰富，构思奇妙，线条细腻而不繁琐，极富浪漫主义色彩。东汉时期，瓦当的使用范围更为广泛，在边远地区也多有发现。这一时期各地的瓦当以当心为一大乳钉的云纹瓦当为主，文

prevalent. The patterns of eaves tiles were various including kylins and phoenixes, flying wild geese, two fish, jade rabbit, toads and dozens of other patterns. Unlike those from the Qin Dynasty with patterns based on real life, although the decorative patterns from the Han Dynasty came from reality, they were rendered in highly artistic exaggeration, rich imagination and creative patterns. Their lines were more delicate but not tedious, sparking with romantic flavor. In the Eastern Han Dynasty (25-220), eaves tiles were so extensively used that they were even found in remote regions. The eaves tiles from various regions during this period were generally decorated with cloud patterns featuring a large stud pattern in the center. The inscription-patterned eaves tiles became fewer than they were in the Western Han Dynasty although their usage was extended geographically.

After the Qin and Han dynasties, bricks and tiles became more extensively used. However, in terms of patterns and the writings, their artistic and academic value began to decline. After the Wei, Jin and the Southern and Northern dynasties (220-581), the Chinese architecture industry began to be infused with foreign characteristics. Glazed tiles emerged

- **骊山风景区**

骊山位于西安临潼区东南，属于秦岭山脉的一个支峰。骊山多温泉，风景秀丽。自三千多年前的西周起就是帝王的游乐宝地，周、秦、汉、唐都曾修建过许多离宫别墅。

Scenic Spot of Lishan Mountain

Located in the southeast of Lintong District in Xi'an City, Lishan Mountain is a peak of the Qinling Mountain. Lishan Mountain has many hot springs and much beautiful scenery and has been a favorite tourist site for emperors since the Western Zhou Dynasty (1046 B.C.-771 B.C.) more than 3,000 years ago. Through the Zhou, Qin, Han and Tang dynasties, many detached palaces and villas were built in this place.

字瓦当较西汉时期数量减少，但使用地域扩大。

秦汉以后，砖瓦的使用更加广泛，但就砖瓦的饰纹和文字而言，无论是艺术价值还是学术价值均日渐衰落。魏晋南北朝以后，中国建筑业开始融入域外特色。北魏时期

during the Northern Wei Dynasty (386-534). Later, glazed bricks and tiles borrowed the applied craft of the tri-color techniques from the Tang Dynasty (618-907) and were greatly promoted in the Sui and Tang dynasties and eventually popularized after the Song Dynasty (960-1279). During the Ming and Qing

出现了琉璃砖瓦，此后琉璃砖瓦又运用唐三彩技艺，在隋唐时期得到推广，宋代以后普及，明清之时，琉璃砖瓦开始在民间使用。琉璃砖瓦成为表现宫殿、宗庙、寺观的庄严与神秘的最佳建材，是皇家大族建筑的必需品。建筑中用琉璃瓦件代替了以前在灰白瓦件上涂色的装饰方法，是中国古代建筑中的一大创新。

dynasties (1368-1911), glazed bricks and tiles were used by the general public and became the best building materials to exhibit the solemn and mystical aura of palaces and temples. They were also necessities for the imperial families and thriving clans. In architecture, glazed tiles replaced the previous method of applying colors on to the pale ware of tiles, which was a major innovation in the architecture of ancient China.

In short, from the Warring States Period (770 B.C.-476 B.C.) through the Qin, Han, Sui, Tang, Song, Yuan, Ming and Qing dynasties, bricks and tiles have been used to construct numerous underground structures (mausoleums), high-platform buildings (palaces), grden

● **陕西法门寺砖塔**
东汉时期佛教传入中国，给中国的砖建筑带来了一个划时代的转变，用砖砌筑的砖塔在中国各地出现，成为砖建筑的一个重要类型。

Brick Tower of Famen Temple in Shaanxi Province
Buddhism was introduced into China in the Eastern Han Dynasty (25-220), which provided Chinese brick buildings with epoch-making changes. Brick towers and brick pagodas emerged across China and became typical types of brick structures.

- 蓝色琉璃瓦屋顶的祈年殿
The Hall of Prayer for Good Harvests with Its Roof Paved with Blue Glazed Tiles

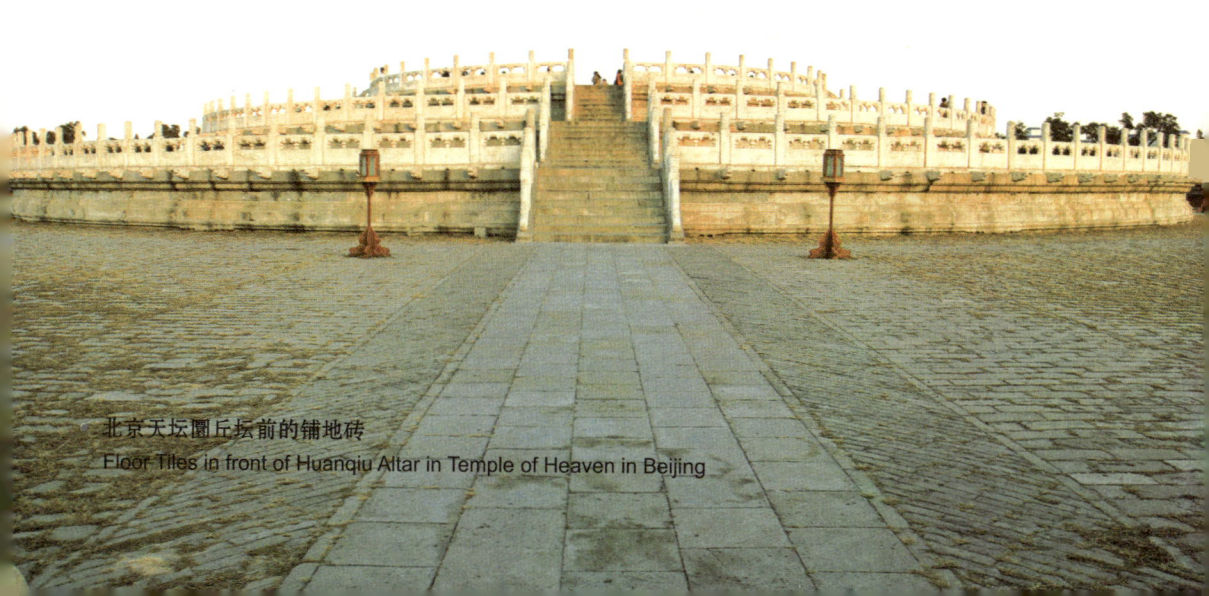

北京天坛圜丘坛前的铺地砖
Floor Tiles in front of Huanqiu Altar in Temple of Heaven in Beijing

- 瓦猫

琉璃瓦上的动物装饰。

Tile Cat

The animal decoration on the glazed tile.

- 北京故宫太和殿龙吻

Loong-head Ornament in the Hall of Supreme Harmony in the Forbidden City

琉璃瓦
Glazed Tile

板瓦：板瓦一般带有弧度，由筒形陶坯四剖或六剖制成。在房屋的顶部铺瓦时，板瓦一般依次仰置于屋顶。

Pan tiles: Pan tiles are generally curved and made by splitting a cylindrical ceramic tube into four or six sections. While paved on rooftops, pan tiles are usually placed inverted in order on the roof.

筒瓦：筒瓦一般为半圆形，制作时为筒状，成坯后一分为二，经烧制成瓦。筒瓦一般覆扣于板瓦与板瓦纵向相接的缝上。

Cylindrical tiles: Cylindrical tiles are generally semi-cylindrical in shape. They are made by splitting the cylindrical tube into two parts prior to the firing. Cylindrical tiles are typically used to cover along the seam between the joined pan tiles.

瓦当：瓦当就是筒瓦下垂的部分。

Eaves tiles: Eaves tiles are the overhanging part of the cylindrical tiles.

• **中国传统房屋的屋顶**

中国古代的瓦分为板瓦和筒瓦两种。

Roof of Traditional Chinese Houses

Tiles in ancient China were categorized into two types: pan tiles and cylindrical tiles.

• 故宫太和殿

砖瓦自从诞生以来，就在中国古代建筑中被广泛使用，是房屋、城墙、道路、陵墓的主要建筑用材。与西方以石头为主要建材的传统建筑有所不同，中国的传统建筑一般以砖、木为主要建材。

The Hall of Supreme Harmony in the Forbidden City in Beijing

Since their very birth, bricks and tiles have been widely used in ancient Chinese architecture as main building materials for houses, city walls, roads and tombs. Unlike the traditional architecture in the West, mostly built of stone, Chinese traditional architecture was generally constructed of bricks and woods.

• 走兽琉璃瓦

走兽琉璃瓦是琉璃瓦的形式之一，一般覆盖在垂脊下端。

The Glazed Tiles with Beasts on Surfaces

The glazed tile with beast is one of the forms, generally vertical ridges covered in lower.

- 故宫的城墙
  The Walls of the Imperial Palace

034

秦砖汉瓦
Qin Bricks and Han Tiles

绿琉璃瓦黄剪边屋顶
Roof with Green Glazed Tiles and Yellow Trimmings

- 琉璃影壁
  Glazed Screen Wall

- 颐和园中的琉璃砖墙
  Glazed Brick Wall in the Summer Palace

• 北京故宫乾清宫内的金砖墁地
Golden Brick Paved Ground at the Hall of Heavenly Purity in the Forbidden City, Beijing

• 金砖

金砖过去专用于北京故宫。明成祖朱棣在建筑故宫时想要一种比石头和金属更坚实的材料，经推荐决定使用苏州陆慕砖窑的砖。这种砖烧制工艺复杂，坚固耐用，在五百年后的今天这些金砖依然完好如初。

Golden Bricks

The golden brick used to be used exclusively in the Forbidden City in Beijing. When Emperor Chengzu of the Ming Dynasty, by the name of Zhu Di, was building the Forbidden City, he had in mind some material harder than stone and tougher than metal. Afer recommendation, he decided to use bricks from brick kiln in Lumu, Suzhou. These bricks have a complex firing process and are hard and durable. They have remained intact for 500 years until today.

• 苏州园林中的建筑用瓦
Tiles Used in Architecture of the Suzhou Gardens

• 北京北海公园内房屋的屋顶
House Roofs at Beihai Park, Beijing

• 山西乔家大院中的影壁
The Screen Wall of Qiao's Grand Courtyard in Shanxi

• 山西王家大院檐下的砖雕
Brick Carving under the Eaves of the Wang's Grand Courtyard in Shanxi Province

● 砖影壁
Brick Screen Wall

● 用砖瓦建造起来的徽州传统民居
Traditional Residential Houses Built with Bricks and Tiles in Huizhou Area

总之，从春秋战国到秦、汉、隋、唐、宋、元、明、清，人们用砖瓦建造了无数的地下建筑（陵墓）、高台建筑（宫殿）、园林建筑、民居建筑，从名都大邑到集镇村落，从台榭宫殿到道观佛塔，从黄土高原的富贾府第到南海之滨的乡村小院，随处都可见到用砖瓦修建的建筑和用砖瓦制成的精美装饰。

architecture and residential houses. From capitals and large cities to small towns and villages, from pavilions and palace buildings to Oaoist temples and Buddhist pagodas, from mansions of wealthy businessmen on the Loess Plateau to the small rural yards on the shore of the South China Sea, the presence of architecture made of bricks and tiles and decorated with beautiful patterns can been spotted everywhere.

砖
Bricks

　　中国古代的砖按种类分主要有素面砖、花纹砖、铭文砖和画像砖。这些造型、种类繁多的砖主要用于屋脊、台基、台阶、地面等，是中国古代建筑的重要组成部分。

The bricks in ancient China are categorized into plain-surface bricks, patterned bricks, inscription-patterned bricks and portrayal bricks. These bricks in a wide range of types were mainly used on roof ridges, platforms, stairs and steps, floors and so on. They are important parts of tradtional Chinese architecture.

> 素面砖

素面砖指表面没有纹饰图案的砖。这类砖多用于铺地、建造房屋等，多起承重作用，一般不用于装饰。

> Plain-surface Bricks

The surfaces of such bricks have no decorated patterns. They are typically used for pavements, building houses and so on to bear loads instead of for decoration.

- 故宫里的铺地砖
Floor Bricks in the Forbidden City

043 | 砖 Bricks

• 故宫里的铺地砖
Floor Bricks in the Forbidden City

● 山西王家大院中的建筑用砖
Bricks Used in the Structures of the Wang's Grand Courtyard in Shanxi Province

> 花纹砖

　　花纹砖指表面饰有各种装饰图案的砖。花纹砖纹饰丰富，砖上通常饰有植物纹、云纹、火焰纹、几何纹、绳纹、菱形纹、回纹、圆形纹、"S"形纹等，有时多种纹样还搭配使用，具有极高的审美价值。

> Patterned Bricks

Patterned bricks are those bricks with surfaces decorated with various patterns. The patterned brick has a wide variety of decorations, usually of vegetation, clouds, flames, geometries, cord, diamonds, fretwork, circular patterns and S-shaped patterns. Sometimes, different patterns were used in combination to achieve high aesthetic results.

- 印模（唐） 图片提供：FOTOE

花纹砖的制作过程是先将要表现的花纹刻在印模（用陶泥烧制成的模板，主要用于青铜器、砖瓦的制造）上，然后将印模打印在未干的砖坯上。印模如果是阴纹，打印在砖坯上就是阳纹；印模如果是阳纹，打印在砖坯上就是阴纹。

Patterned Print Mold (Tang Dynasty, 618-907)

To make patterned bricks, featured patterns need to be carved on the print mold (a mold made of fired ceramic clay for the production of bronze ware or bricks), followed by pressing the print mold onto the not-yet-dried adobe. If the print mold is carved in intaglio, the pattern printed on the surface of the adobe will show in relief, and vice versa.

• 花纹空心砖
Patterned Hollow Bricks

• 龙纹空心砖（汉）

空心砖盛行于战国和秦汉时期，体积一般比较庞大，空心，又称"空腹砖""空砖"。空心砖一般为长方形砖，也有门楣砖、支柱砖和三角形砖等。空心砖通常外印各种纹饰，内容有卫士、老虎、朱雀、飞雁、舞乐、骑射、田猎等。空心砖也常作铺地砖用，多用于铺筑宫殿、官署的踏步与台阶，以增添端庄雄伟的气氛。另外在陵墓中也用空心砖建造椁室，以替代木制棺椁。

Loong-patterned Hollow Brick (Han Dynasty, 206 B.C.-220 A.D.)

Hollow bricks were prevalent during the Warring States Period (475 B.C.-221 B.C.) and the Qin and Han dynasties (221 B.C.-220 A.D.). They were usually massive in size and hollow inside, thus also known as empty-stomach bricks or empty bricks. Hollow bricks are mostly rectangular, although there are lintel-based hollow bricks, pillar-used hollow bricks and triangular hollow bricks. The external surfaces of hollow bricks were usually decorated with various patterns such as guards, tigers, sparrows, flying wild geese, dancing, horseback shooting and hunting. Hollow bricks were often used to pave the steps and stairs in palaces or government offices to boast a dignified and majestic atmosphere. Beyond that, hollow bricks were also used to build the coffin chamber as a replacement for wood coffins.

- **饰有纹饰的铺地砖**

  铺地砖一般呈正方形或长方形，也叫"方砖"或"长方砖"，多为素面砖，但仍有一些铺地砖饰有多种纹饰。

  Patterned Floor Bricks

  Floor bricks are generally square or rectangular in shape, hence known as square bricks or rectangular bricks. Most of them are plain-surface bricks, but there are still various decorated patterns on some floor bricks.

- **几何纹砖（汉）**

  Geometric-patterned Brick (Han Dynasty, 206 B.C.-220 A.D.)

- **方格纹砖（汉）**

  Rectangle-patterned Brick (Han Dynasty, 206 B.C.-220 A.D.)

• **画像空心砖中的局部图案（汉）**

西汉时，空心砖在题材、内容、构图等方面有了更大的发展，不再是单纯的建筑材料，也成为富有艺术价值的陶制工艺品。这两幅图都是汉代画像空心砖上的图案。这些反映当时人们生活的图案为我们了解汉代社会风情提供了实物资料。

Part of Portrayal Patterns on Hollow Bricks (Han Dynasty, 206 B.C.-220 A.D.)

Hollow bricks acquired considerable progress during the Western Han Dynasty (206 B.C.-25 A.D.) in terms of their themes, contents and compositions. They were no longer simple building materials, but rather ceramic ware with rich artistic values. These two pictures show parts of the portrayal-patterned hollow bricks from the Han Dynasty (206 B.C.-220 A.D.). They reflect the lives of people at that time and provide us with real information to understand the social customs in the Han Dynasty.

- 浮雕凤纹方砖（唐）
  Relief Phoenix Design Brick(Tang Dynasty,618-907)

- 浮雕莲花蔓草纹方砖（唐）
  Relief Lotus and Weeds Patterns Brick (Tang Dynasty, 618-907)

> 铭文砖

铭文砖上一般刻有文字，铭文多为玺印式，一般有纪年、吉文、名号，文字字体有篆、隶、楷等多种形式，有些文字字体瘦劲古朴，

> Inscription-patterned Bricks

Inscription-patterned bricks are usually carved with writings. The inscriptions on the bricks are generally stamped patterns via the seal in the forms of years and dates, blessing words and names. The

- **秦小篆体十二字砖（秦）**

此砖正面以凸线分为十二个方格，每格内有一阳文秦篆，文字是"海内皆臣，岁登成熟，道毋饥人"，意思是普天下的人都是秦朝的臣民，五谷丰登，路上没有饥饿的人。这是秦朝都城的宫殿用砖。

Inscription-patterned Bricks with 12 Characters in Small Seal Scripts of Qin (Qin Dynasty, 221 B.C.-206 B.C.)

The front of this brick is divided into 12 squares in relief lines. Each square includes a character in relief in the small seal scripts. The text reads: "All the people across the country are subjects of the Qin Dynasty and with the abundant harvest of crops, there are no starving people on the streets." This was a brick for constructing palaces from the capital of the Qin Dynasty.

极具研究价值。铭文砖中的秦砖十分罕见,汉砖相对较多。

writings may come in the seal scripts, clerical scripts, regular scripts and others. Some writings are slim but forceful and quaint and possess great value for study. Text-patterned bricks are rare among the unearthed Qin bricks. On the other hand, they were quite common in Han bricks.

- **十六字铭文砖(汉)**

  这块十六字铭文砖的铭文为"海内皆臣,岁登成熟,道毋饥人,践此万岁"。据说此砖是汉朝皇帝每年庆贺丰收时用的"红地毯",只供皇帝踩踏。铭文内容表达了汉代最高统治者希望社会安定统一,经济繁荣发展,人民生活富裕的强烈愿望。同时,他们也希望自己的统治能够万代相传,永世不衰。

Inscription-patterned Brick with 16 Characters (Han Dynasty, 206 B.C.-220 A.D.)

The inscription on this inscription-patterned brick with 16 characters reads: "All the people across the country are subjects of the Han Dynasty and with the abundant harvests of crops piled as high as the city wall; no starving people are seen on the streets. May this last forever." It is said that this brick was used as the red carpet for emperors of the Han Dynasty exclusively during the annual harvest celebration. The content expressed the strong wishes of the highest rulers of the Han Dynasty to realize social stability, national unity, prosperous economic development and a wealthy life for people. Meanwhile, it also expressed hopes that his rule would continue from generation to generation and last forever.

中国书法的书体

中国书法是汉字的书写艺术。中国书法依托汉字发展出5种书体,分别是:楷书、行书、草书、隶书、篆书。中国书法有丰富完整和一脉相承的理论体系,很多高水平的书法作品以书信、诗词手稿、碑文、墓志铭、碑匾、屏风和室内装饰品等形式存在,是琴、棋、书、画四艺之一。在中国古代,书艺有非常高的参与程度,受到中国古代帝王和知识分子的重视。一定的书法水平是中国古代知识分子的基本素质之一,一般知识分子都会付出不同程度的努力学习书法,因此出现了数量众多的书法家。自秦汉以来,各个朝代都有相当多的书法作品流传于世，其中最优秀者会成为皇室、贵族和文人珍贵的收藏品。中国历史上著名的书法家有王羲之、颜真卿、柳公权等。

Different Scripts in Chinese Calligraphy

Chinese calligraphy is the art of writing Chinese characters. Progressing along with Chinese characters, Chinese calligraphy has developed five different writing styles: the regular script, the running script, the cursive script, the clerical script and the seal script. Chinese calligraphy encompasses a rich, complete and continuous line of theoretical system. Many hight-level works of calligraphy exist in the form of letters, poetry manuscripts, inscriptions, epitaphs, monument plaques, screens, indoor decorations and the like. Chinese calligraphy, together with the *Guqin*-playing, chess and painting, constitute the Four Arts. In ancient China, calligraphy entertained a very high level of participation and was highly emphasized by ancient Chinese rulers and intellectuals. Acquiring a certain level of calligraphy standard was a basic cultural quality required for ancient Chinese intellectuals. Generally, intellectuals in ancient China had to make varying degrees of effort in order to learn the skills of calligraphy. Therefore, there have been a great number of calligraphers in China. Throughout the history since the Qin and Han dynasties (221 B.C.-220 A.D.), a considerable quantity of calligraphy works have been passed down. The most outstanding ones would often become valuable collections of the imperial families, noblemen or literati. Some of the illustrious calligraphers in the development of Chinese calligraphy include Wang Xizhi, Yan Zhenqing and Liu Gongquan.

● 晋代王羲之《快雪时晴帖》
Calligraphy *Sunny after Snow* by Wang Xizhi in the Jin Dynasty (265-420)

- 铭文砖（明）
The Inscription-patterned Brick
(Ming Dynasty, 1368-1644)

- 铭文城砖
扬州唐代罗城遗址出土。
The Inscription-patterned Brick
It was unearthed from the Luocheng site of the Tang Dynasty in Yangzhou.

- 铭文城砖（唐）
The Inscription-patterned Brick (Tang Dynasty, 618-907)

• 铭文砖
Inscription-patterned Brick

• 南京明城墙的铭文砖（图片提供：FOTOE）

南京城墙曾是世界上最长的一座砖砌城墙。为了保证质量，朱元璋要求每一块砖侧面都印上烧造地从知府、知县到乡里各级督工、监造官员以及砖工、窑匠的姓名。

The Inscription-patterned Brick of the Nanjing Ming-dynasty City Wall

The city wall of Nanjing was once the longest brick wall in the world. In order to ensure the quality, Zhu Yuanzhang, Emperor Hongwu of the Ming Dynasty, ordered that the side of each brick be printed with the names of taskmasters and supervision officers, as well as the names of the brick craftsmen and potters.

> 画像砖

> Portrayal Bricks

画像砖是中国古代用于宫殿或者墓室建筑的装饰画砖，是一种表面有模印、彩绘或雕刻图案的建筑用砖。它作为一种装饰性建筑构件，始于战国晚期，兴盛于两汉，

Portrayal bricks are the bricks carved with paintings or drawings and were used in imperial palaces or tomb buildings in ancient China. It is a constructional type of brick with prints, color-paintings or carved patterns on the surface. As

- 荆轲刺秦故事画像砖（汉）

荆轲刺秦是发生在战国末期秦军征战六国时期的一件非常著名的历史事件。燕国太子丹派刺客荆轲前去刺杀秦王嬴政。荆轲带着燕国最肥沃土地的地图和叛秦将领的首级，前往秦国。秦王在咸阳宫召见了他。荆轲借献地图之际刺杀秦王，不中，被秦王杀死。

Portrayal Brick Depicting the Story of Jing Ke's Assassination of the King of the Qin State(Han Dynasty, 206 B.C.-220 A.D.)

The story of Jing Ke's assassination of the king of the Qin state was a historical event that occurred during the late Warring States Period, when the Qin army campaigned to conquer the other Six States. Prince Dan of the Yan State recruited an assassin, Jing Ke, to assassinate Ying Zheng, king of the Qin State. Jing Ke brought a scrolled map of the most fertile lands in the Yan State as well as the head of the rebel general from Qin and headed to Qin. The king of Qin summoned him up at the palace in Xianyang. Jing Ke took the chance of offering the map and attempted to assassinate the king of Qin with a dagger hidden in the scroll but failed. He was later killed by the king of Qin.

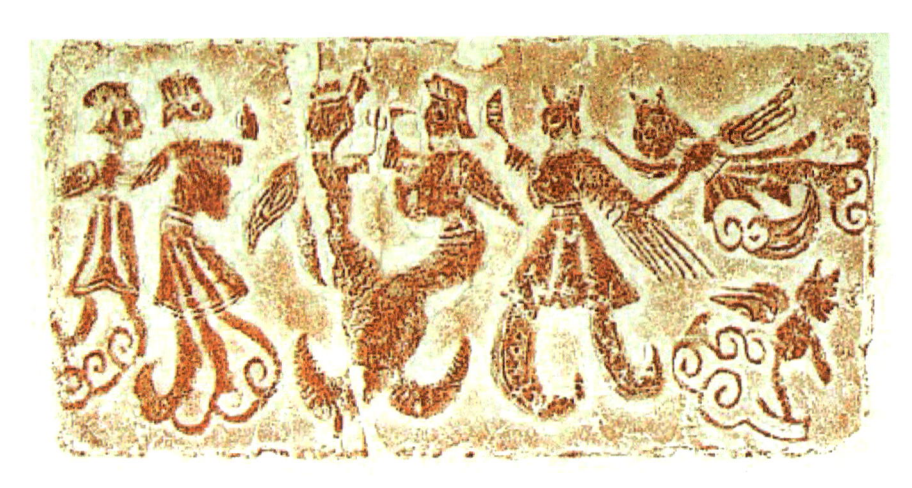

- 伏羲女娲画像砖拓片（汉）

河南郏县出土的伏羲女娲画像砖描绘了神话中伏羲、女娲兄妹成婚繁衍人类的故事。该画像砖长39厘米，宽19厘米，厚度为4厘米，砖面涂有护胎粉，属高浮雕工艺。图中伏羲、女娲居中偏左（戴葵花帽者为女娲），两尾相交，尾粗有鳞，敛羽相顾，身后有长翅，无脚，手中分别执矩和规。整个画面除伏羲和女娲外，还有五个羽人伴其左右。左有两个羽人，穿褶裙，腿部已化成蛇尾状，向内卷曲成云纹符号。右侧有三个羽人，面向二神的一个羽人有双尾，并有铠状纹饰；右上方的羽人呈飞翔状，身下祥云数朵，向二神飞来；右下方的小羽人脚踏祥云向右侧飞去。汉代的雕刻、绘画水平由此可见一斑。

The Rubbing of Portrayal Brick of Fuxi and Nüwa (Han Dynasty, 206 B.C.-220 A.D.)

The portrayal brick of Fuxi and Nüwa excavated from Jiaxian County in Henan Province depicts the mythical tale of Fuxi and Nüwa, who got married and repopulated the world with humans. This portrayal brick is 39 cm long, 19 cm wide and 4 cm thick, with a protective powder covering its surface. It's a work of art produced through high-relief techniques. In the portrayal, Fuxi and Nüwa are positioned in the center a little to the left (the figure in a sunflower hat being Nüwa). With their thick and scaly tails interwined, they face each other, long wings closed on their backs, with no feet and holding a ruler and a compass in their hands. In addition to Fuxi and Nüwa, there are another five feather-winged individuals by their side, two of them on the left wearing pleated skirts with legs transformed into the shape of snake tails and curled inward into patterns of cloud symbols. Among the three feather-winged individuals on the right, the one facing the two deities has two tails with armor patterns. The feather-winged one on the upper-right is flying toward the two deities, a number of clouds floating beneath him. The little feather-winged one on the lower right is stepping on the cloud and flying toward the right. The high level of sculpture and painting in the Han Dynasty is evidenced here.

- **西王母画像砖（东汉）** (图片提供：FOTOE)

在中国古代典籍中，西王母是个神秘人物，住在遥远的昆仑山瑶池畔。在四川、山东、河南、辽宁等地都出土过与西王母有关的汉代画像砖。

Portrayal Brick of the Queen Mother of the West (Eastern Han Dynasty, 25-220)

In ancient Chinese classics, the Queen Mother of the West is a mysterious character. She lives on the bank of the remote Jasper Pond in Kunlun Mountains. The portrayal bricks of the Queen Mother of the West from the Han Dynasty have ever been discovered in Sichuan, Shandong, Henan, Liaoning and other regions.

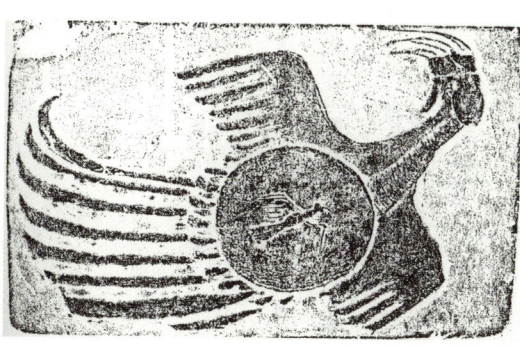

- **日神羽人画像砖和月神羽人画像砖拓片** (图片提供：FOTOE)

这两块东汉画像砖上的图案跟中国古人崇拜太阳和光明有关。

Rubbings of Portrayal Brick of Feather-winged Sun God and Portrayal Brick of Feather-winged Moon God

Both of these portrayal bricks from the Eastern Han Dynasty are related to the sun-worship and light-worship of the ancient Chinese people.

"弋射图"：池塘水波涟涟，群鱼游动，莲蓬挺立于水面，一群水鸭惊慌失措，仓皇飞散。池畔两位猎人侧身跪地，向天劲射，身姿健美。

Picture of Arrow-shooting: Under the rippled surface of the pond, shoals of fish swim. The lotus seedpods stretch high above the water surface and a flock of teals hurries up in panic and scatters about. Two hunters are kneeling in magnificent body postures on their side by the pond, aiming their bows and arrows in the sky.

"收获图"：有农夫正挥镰收割，其中左侧的一组三人弯腰小心翼翼地割稻穗，右侧一组二人高高地举起镰刀砍稻茎，最左侧一人荷担而立，似乎为送饭者。

Picture of Harvesting: Farmers are harvesting with sickles. A group of three on the left side is bending over as they carefully cut down stalks of rice. Another group of two on the right have their sickles raised to chop down rice stems. The single one on the far left stands there holding a hoe and seems to be the meal deliverer in the field.

- 弋射收获画像砖拓片（汉）（图片提供：FOTOE）

"弋射收获画像砖"是汉画像砖中的杰作，在一块砖面上分上下两部分绘画，上面描绘的是池边弋射，下面则是田间收获。这是汉代人们劳动生活的真实写照。

The Rubbing of Portrayal Brick of Arrow Shooting and Harvesting (Han Dynasty, 206 B.C.-220 A.D.)

The Portrayal Brick of Arrow Shooting and Harvesting is a masterpiece from the Han Dynasty. The surface of the brick is divided into two sections. The picture on the top shows people shooting by the side of a pond, while the picture on the bottom depicts a scene of harvesting in the field. It is a true portrayal of the laboring life of the people in the Han Dynasty.

东汉时达到了艺术的高峰，宋元时期仍有使用。

　　画像砖的形制大致有大型空心砖和较小的实心砖两种。前者最早出现于战国晚期，后者则流行于汉代，尤其在东汉以后的墓葬中大量出现，主要用于装饰墓室的墙壁。汉人重视死者墓葬，"事死如事生"，故赋予墓室以死者身后住所的象征意义，墓室就是墓主人生前生活环境的缩影。厚葬与"死即是生"的观念吻合，因此画像砖在汉代墓葬中发现数量最多，并有着丰富的表现内容。这种画像砖集雕刻和绘画于一体，成为一种杰出的中国传统艺术品。

　　秦代画像砖多为巨大的空心砖和条形砖，主要用作宫殿的台阶，其中以秦旧都栎阳（今陕西阎良）和秦都咸阳出土的画像砖最为精美。

　　汉代画像砖形制多样，绘画内容包罗了汉代政治、经济、文化、民俗各个方面。这些砖上通常绘有楼阁、桥梁、车骑、仪仗、乐舞、百戏、祥瑞、异兽、神话故事、奇花异草等，其图案精彩，主题丰富，画技古朴，深刻反映了两汉的

a decorative building component, the portrayal bricks appeared in the late Warring States Period, flourished during the Han Dynasty, and reached its artistic peak during the Eastern Han Dynasty. It continued to be used during the Song and Yuan dynasties.

Portrayal bricks generally come in two different shapes: large hollow bricks and smaller solid bricks. The former first appeared in the late Warring States Period. The latter prevailed during the Han Dynasty. After the Eastern Han Dynasty in particular, they were used in large quantities for tombs to decorate grave walls. The people of Han placed emphasis on the tomb of the deceased because of the concept that matters in death are equivalent to matters of life. Therefore, the tomb of the deceased was endowed with the symbolic meaning that it was the residence of the deceased after death. In other words, the tomb epitomized the living environment of the deceased. The idea of elaborate funerals was consistent with the concept that death is life. Therefore, those tombs from the Han Dynasty house the highest quantity of unearthed portrayal bricks with rich content. With carving and painting combined together, portrayal bricks have

左上：一只独木舟，一人撑舟，舟头伏一猎犬，正注视水中。

Top left: A single canoe carries an individual holding a pole and a hunting dog crouch at the bow staring at the water.

左中：有一池塘，池内有众多的莲蓬和荷叶，数只水禽在水中游戏，水面上泛着两只独木舟。

Center left: There is a pond with many lotus seedpods and lotus leaves. Several waterfowl swim in the pond and two canoes float on the surface of the water.

- **采莲、渔猎画像砖（东汉）** (图片提供：FOTOE)
  这块画像砖为长方体，采用模制高浮雕的手法。
  Portrayal Brick of Lotus Gathering, Fishing and Hunting (Eastern Han Dynasty, 25-220)
  Rectangular in shape, this portrayal brick was molded through high-relief techniques.

左下：一只独木舟上，一人撑舟，一人张弓欲射，另一人在船头俯身采莲。

Bottom left: A single canoe is punted by an individual while the second individual is holding his bow and arrow ready for shooting, and the other individual at the bow of the canoe is leaning over to pick lotus flowers.

右图：这是池岸，岸上有树，树上有调皮的小猴和飞禽，树下一人正持弓箭仰射树上飞禽，整个画面充满浓厚的生活气息。

Right: The bank of the pond has trees with mischievous monkeys and birds on them. A person is under the tree, ready to shoot his arrow at the birds in the trees. The entire picture is full of a strong sense of life.

左下角:赤膊的盐工在高耸的井架上忙碌着,利用滑车装置从井下汲取卤水,然后通过枧筒注入长灶上的盐釜中。灶下有工人不断添柴烧火,以将灶上盐釜中的卤水熬成盐。

Bottom-left corner: Shirtless salt workers are busy working on the well derrick drawing salt brine from the underground through a pulley device. The barrel tube then pours the salt brine into the salt oven above the long stove. Workers are constantly adding firewood under the stove in order to boil the salt brine on the stove to produce dry salt.

右上角:盐场后面就是层叠的山峦,多种鸟兽出没于山林之中。

Upper-right corner: Behind the salt field lie the cascading mountains, where a variety of birds and animals appear in the mountain woods.

正中:为了烧旺盐灶,不断有工人从山中背来成捆的木柴。

Center: In order to keep the fire ablaze for the salt oven, workers keep carrying bundles of firewood from the mountains.

- 盐井画像砖拓片

这块出土于成都羊子山一号墓的盐井画像砖,使两千年前井盐生产的景象重现于世。它细致地刻画了汉代井盐生产的情况,是研究中国古代盐业史难得的实证。

The Rubbing of Portrayal Brick of Salt Wells

This portrayal brick of salt wells was unearthed from Tomb NO.1 at Yangzi Mountatin in Chengdu. It reproduces the vivid scene of salt production 2,000 years ago and portrays a detailed picture of salt production during the Han Dynasty (206 B.C.-220 A.D.). It is valuable evidence for studying the salt industry history in ancient China.

社会风情。根据题材的不同，大致可以分为以下几类：表现当时神话传说的画像砖，诸如伏羲、女娲等；反映农业、副业、手工业和商业的画像砖，如播种、收割、舂米、桑园、酿酒、盐井、采莲、市井等，内容丰富，题材广泛，将汉代人的生活状况真实地保存了来；表现墓主身份、经历和享乐生活的画像砖，诸如车骑出巡图、执剑起舞图等。此类画像砖的墓主多为当地的豪强显贵，从一定角度反映了汉代宴饮、庭院、庖厨、乐舞、百戏、车马、出行等民俗。还有表现

become an outstanding form of Chinese traditional art.

Portrayal bricks in the Qin Dynasty are typically large hollow bricks and bar bricks. They were mainly used as steps in palaces. Among them, the most exquisite examples were those excavated from Yueyang, the old Qin capital, and Xianyang, the capital of the Qin Dynasty.

Although varied in different shapes, portrayal bricks from the Han Dynasty encompassed all aspects of the dynasty including politics, economy, culture, folklore and other aspects. They were usually decorated with patterns of pavilions, bridges, carriages,

- **庖厨图画像砖片拓片（汉）**

(图片提供：FOTOE)

在中国许多地方的汉墓中都发现了庖厨图，主要内容大致相同，略有差别，这反映了汉代地方饮食习俗的基本一致性。从众多庖厨图来看，汉代对肉食的加工主要有烤炙和蒸煮，炊具主要是釜和甑。

The Rubbing of Portrayal Brick of a Kitchen (Han Dynasty, 206 B.C.-220 A.D.)

Portrayals of kitchens can be found in many tombs dating back to the Han Dynasty. Their contents are mostly identical with slight differences, showing the consistency in the local customs of diet during the Han Dynasty. Judged from many kitchen portrayals, meat was usually cauterized or steamed in the major cookware named *Fu* and *Zeng* during the Han Dynasty.

- 春米画像砖（汉）

  春米就是将稻谷去壳的过程。先秦一般用杵和臼舂米，汉代先后出现了用于加工谷物的脚踏碓、畜力碓和水力碓。脚踏碓在汉代应用普遍，其效率十倍于手工杵舂。这块画像砖完整而精细地刻画了脚踏碓的结构和操作方法。

  Portrayal Brick of Husking (Han Dynasty, 206 B.C.-220 A.D.)

  Husking is the process of hulling the chaff off rice. Mortars and pestles were generally used for the purpose in the Pre-Qin Period, but tools such as foot pestles, animal-powered pestles and hydraulic-powered pestles appeared successively to help to process grain in the Han Dynasty (206 B.C.-220 A.D.). Foot pestles were prevalent in the Han Dynasty with an efficiency 10 times more than that of manual pestles. This piece of portrayal brick provides a complete and detailed portrayal of the structure of the foot pestle and its operation method.

- 酿酒画像砖（汉）

  中国是世界上最早掌握酿酒技术的国家之一，大约在新石器时代就出现了酒。酒的出现与农业文明关系密切，除食用外有多余的谷物为酿酒提供了可能。这块画像砖反映了汉代人们酿酒的情景。

  Portrayal Brick of Wine-making (Han Dynasty, 206 B.C.-220 A.D.)

  China is one of the first countries in the world to master wine-making techniques. Wine made its debut in around the Neolithic Age (approximately 8,000 years ago). Its appearance was closely related to the agricultural civilization, which made it possible to turn excessive grain into wine. This portrayal brick reflects a scene of making wine in the Han Dynasty.

左中：此为过厅，内院有双鹤对舞，反映了汉代养鹤的习俗。

Center left: This is the passage hall. Two cranes are dancing in the inner court, revealing the custom of residents in the Han Dynasty raising cranes.

左上方：此为堂屋，堂上置酒樽，主客对酌。

Upper left: This is the main hall, where the hosts and guests share wine.

正中：画像上的宅院四周有厢房环布，院中由厢房隔成两部分。

Center: The courtyard in the portrayal is surrounded by wing rooms and divided by the wing rooms into two parts.

右上方：堂右有门通右后院，这里建有一座高大的望楼，下层有梯，上层有窗，供人在此眺望。

Upper right: The door to the right of the main hall leads to the right courtyard in the back, where a tall lookout tower stands. There is a ladder on the lower level, and windows are seen on the upper level for people overlooking the whole area.

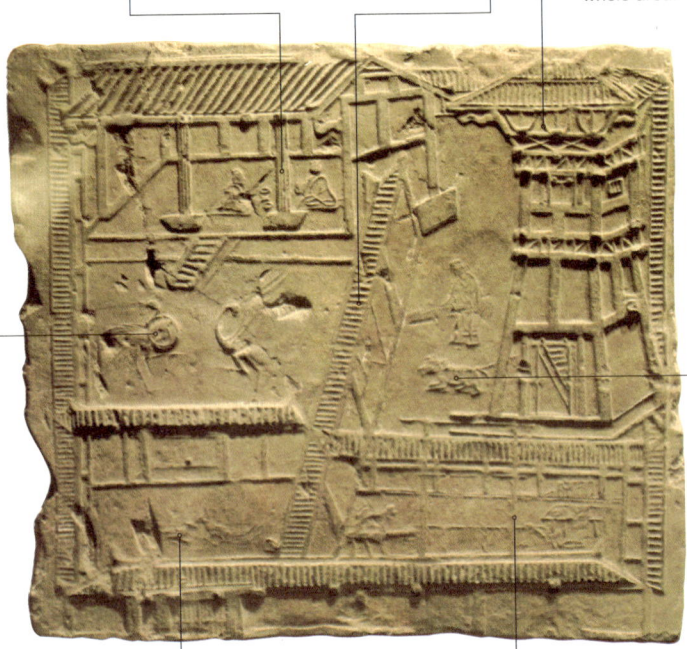

右中：楼下系一猛犬，仆役正执帚扫地。

Center right: A fierce dog is tied downstairs. Servants are sweeping the rooms.

• 宅院画像砖（汉）

此宅院画像砖出土于四川成都羊子山。

Portrayal Brick of Courtyard (Han Dynasty, 206 B.C.-220 A.D.)

This portrayal brick of courtyard was unearthed from Yangzi Mountain in Chengdu, Sichuan Province.

左下方：大门在左院的左下方，门内有两鸡相斗。

Bottom left: The main entrance is located in the left courtyard at the bottom left, where two chickens are fighting each other.

右下方：一小跨院，院内有井，设案、灶、厨具等，符合古诗中"东厨具肴膳"的描述。

Bottom right: A small stretch of the yard has a well, where a table, stove and kitchenware catch the eye. This is in line with the descriptions in an ancient poem that "delicacies are cooked in the east kitchen".

- **辎车画像砖（东汉）**

汉代辎车的车厢一般两侧开窗，后方开门，车盖多呈篷形。车厢分为前、后两部分，主人坐在后舆，御者在前舆中执马。汉代辎车主要供妇女乘坐，史书中多处记载皇帝的母亲、皇后或后妃出门必乘辎车。此画像砖所表现的是汉代有钱人家的妇女乘坐辎车的情景。

Portrayal Brick of a Logistic Wagon (Eastern Han Dynasty, 25-220)

The logistic wagon in the Han Dynasty often had windows on both sides and a door on the back, covered by a canopy-shaped hood. The wagon is divided into two compartments. The owner rides in the back while the charioteer is seated in the front controlling the horse. The logistic wagon in the Han Dynasty was used primarily to carry women. It was recorded in many historic books that emperors' mothers, empresses and concubines always rode the logistic wagons when going out. This portrayal brick depicts a typical scene of women from wealthy families riding the logistic wagon in the Han Dynasty.

- **宴饮画像砖拓片（东汉）** （图片提供：FOTOE）

汉代人宴饮成风。7个衣冠楚楚的人正捧盘举杯，饮酒作乐，这是汉代贵族们宴会饮酒的情景。

The Rubbing of Portrayal Brick of a Banquet (Eastern Han Dynasty, 25-220)

The people of the Han Dynasty had the habit of drinking during banquets. Seven well-dressed individuals are holding plates and cups, enjoying a drink. This is a typical scene of the nobles of the Han Dynasty at a banquet.

flags, musical dances, acrobatics, auspicious signs, animals, myths, extraordinary flowers and rare herbs. Their splendid designs, rich themes and plain and classic drawing techniques mirrored the social customs of the Western and Eastern Han dynasties (206 B.C.-220 A.D.). Based on their different themes, the portrayal bricks can be roughly divided into the following categories: those depicting the myths and legends of that time, such as Fuxi and Nüwa, both of whom were legendary figures of ancient China; those reflecting agriculture,

左上方：席上一男子向前伸展长袖，势欲起舞；一高髻女子正在吹排箫伴奏。

Upper left: A male has his long-sleeve stretched forward as if he's ready to dance. A female with tall hair buns is playing a panpipe as musical accompaniment.

右上方：一人耍弄弹丸，七弹齐飞；一人舞剑，并用肘部耍弄瓶子。

Upper right: A person is playing throwing balls, with seven of them flying out at the same time. Another one is sword-dancing while using his elbow to juggle the bottles.

左中：有大小二鼎，杯盘已撤，宴罢开始歌舞。

Center left: With big and small cooking vessels, cups and plates removed, the banquet is followed by singing and dancing.

左下方：二人共坐一席，同吹排箫。

Bottom left: Two individuals are sitting on a shared mat while playing the panpipes at the same time.

右下方：一高髻细腰乐伎高扬长袖而舞，一人击鼓伴舞。

Bottom right: A slender-waisted female performer with tall hair buns is waving long sleeves while dancing, while another is drumming.

- 观伎画像砖（汉）（图片提供：FOTOE）

汉代的乐舞百戏表演多是在筵宴的场面上，此画像砖就生动地表现了汉代这种宴宾的习俗：一男一女席地而坐，在鼓、排箫的伴奏声中，欣赏艺人跳丸、跳瓶、巾舞等表演。此画面生活气息浓郁，艺术形象生动，为研究汉代的乐舞百戏艺术提供了珍贵的资料。

Portrayal Brick of Watching Performances (Eastern Han Dynasty, 25-220)

Musical dancing and acrobatic performances were commonly held at banquets during the Han Dynasty. This portrayal brick vividly depicts this custom of watching performances at a banquet. A man and a woman are sitting on the floor watching performers ball jumping, bottle jumping and towel dancing to the tune of the drumming and panpipe music. This pictorial scene is teeming with liveliness and vivid artistic images. It provides valuable information for the study of dances and acrobatics in the Han Dynasty.

● **三骑吏画像砖（东汉）** （图片提供：FOTOE）
四川成都出土。画面从右往左有三吏骑马前行。三人均头戴冠帽，三马皆短鬃，结伴奔驰向前。
Portrayal Brick of Three Officials on Horses (Eastern Han Dynasty, 25-220)
Unearthed in Chengdu, Sichuan Province, the portrayal comprises three officials riding horses from the right to the left. The three officials are wearing crown caps and the three horses have short horsehair, dashing forward abreast.

当时社会生活的，诸如以市集、杂技、讲学授经、尊贤养老等为主题的画像砖。另外也有龙、牛、虎、马、鹿、鱼、象等动物题材的画像砖。

到了南北朝时期，佛教盛行，它不仅极大地影响了当时的思想文化领域，也影响到各个艺术领域。与以往的表现内容不同，画像砖从汉代传统题材里拓展开来，出现了

sideline businesses, handicrafts, and commercial businesses in the images of planting, harvesting, husking, mulberry fields, wine brewing, salt wells, lotus picking, marketplaces and so on. They all featured rich content and an extensive range of subjects, having realistically preserved the lifestyles of the people of the Han Dynasty; and those highlighting the social status of the deceased hosts of the tombs, their experience and

• 讲学画像砖拓片（汉）

（图片提供：FOTOE）

汉代讲学画像砖生动地再现了讲授儒经时的情景。图中左边形象较高大者为老师，其余为弟子。老师循循善诱，弟子毕恭毕敬。此画像砖反映了汉代的教育情况。

The Rubbing of Portrayal Brick of Lecturing (Han Dynasty, 206 B.C.-220 A.D.)

This portrayal brick from the Han Dynasty vividly represents the scene of a lecture on Confucian classics. The taller figure on the left is the teacher, and the rest are all disciples. The teacher seems to be giving patient guidance, while the disciples are reverent and respectful. This portrayal brick reflects an education scene in the Han Dynasty.

• 炼丹画像砖（东汉）

东汉道教兴盛，此画像砖表现的就是炼丹的场景。

Portrayal Brick of Alchemy (Eastern Han Dynasty, 25-220)

Taoism flourished in the Eastern Han Dynasty (25-220). This portrayal brick shows a scene of alchemy being practiced.

大量反映佛教内容的精美作品。

画像砖在隋唐之后逐渐衰落，虽然在各地仍有画像砖出现，但内容日益形式化和简单化。北宋以后，在原先模印画像砖的基础上，

joyful lives, illustrated in pictures of carriage tours as well as ball playing and sword dancing. The deceased hosts of tombs with such portrayal bricks were generally local dignitaries. In a certain way, these portrayal bricks

● 执盾兵士画像砖（东汉）

两幅画面中，都是一列士兵带着剑、弓、长矛或盾牌在列队出行，它们为了解汉代军事情况提供了图像参考。

Portrayal Brick of Shielded Soldiers (Eastern Han Dynasty, 25-220)

Both pictures display a marching procession of soldiers holding swords, bows, spears or shields. They serve as image references for understanding the military situation in the Han Dynasty.

又兴起了以雕刻为主要手段的砖雕艺术。元代以后，画像砖逐渐退出了历史舞台。

reflect various folk customs of the Han Dynasty, such as feasts, the courtyard, the kitchen, musical dances, acrobatics, carriage and horses, traveling and the like. Some portrayal bricks also express the social life at that time, such as the themes of the market, acrobatics, lectures and the courtesy of respecting the talented and elders. In addition, there were also portrayal bricks in the images of loongs, oxen, tigers, horses, deer, fish, elephants and so forth.

During the Northern and Southern dynasties (420-589) when Buddhism prevailed, it not only exerted significant influence on the thought and culture at that time, but also had the impact on to a variety of arts. The contents of portrayal bricks began to differ from the past and were expanded from the confines of the traditional themes of the Han Dynasty. Large amounts of exquisite works were seen reflecting the contents of Buddhism.

Portrayal bricks gradually declined after the Sui and Tang dynasties (581-907) although they were still around in various regions. However, the content

• 战马出行画像砖（南朝）（图片提供：FOTOE）

出土于河南的这块画像砖，显示了当时已有防御性很强的重装甲骑兵部队。

Portrayal Brick of War-horses Traveling (Southern Dynasties, 420-589)

Unearthed in Henan Province, this portrayal brick shows that there was a strongly defensive armored cavalry at that time.

of portrayal bricks became increasingly formalized and simplified. After the Northern Song Dynasty (960-1127), the hand-carved art of sculptured bricks branched out of the original printed portrayal bricks and came into its own existence. After the Yuan Dynasty (1206-1368), portrayal bricks were gradually phased out.

• 鹿首浮雕画像砖（汉）

鹿首线条流畅，极富动感，是研究汉代绘画、雕刻难得的实物。

Portrayal Brick of a Deer Head in Relief (Han Dynasty, 206 B.C.-220 A.D.)

With smooth and dynamic lines, this deer-head brick is a rare item for studying the sculpturing and painting arts in the Han Dynasty.

- 双蛇画像砖（汉）
  Portrayal Brick of Double Snake (Han Dynasty, 206 B.C.-220 A.C.)

- 浮雕画像砖（汉）
  Relief Portrayal Brick (Han Dynasty, 206 B.C.-220 A.D.)

右下方：楼下端坐二人，他们可能是管理市集的官吏，当时称为"市令""市长"或"市丞"。

Bottom right: Two people sitting downstairs. They may be the officials in charge of the marketplace, known as market officials, market officers or market governors at that time.

图中：市楼与市门之间为交易场所，有列肆坐售的，也有摆摊贩卖的。

Center: The area between the market building and the market gate is the trading venue, where lines of shops or stands can be seen.

左边：有一门，门旁题有"东市门"。

Left: There is a gate with the title East Market Gate beside it.

右边：此为两层的市楼，楼门题有"市楼"二字。市楼是管理市肆的官署所在地。由于市楼是市内最高大的建筑，开市时在市楼上可以观察并监视市内交易的情景。市楼上悬鼓，每日开市和闭市都要击鼓。

Right: This is a two-floor market building. On the door is written Market Building. Since the market building is where the city officials who managed the market were located, it is the tallest building in the city from where all trading activity can be easily observed and monitored from the upper floor when the market is open. There is a drum hung on the upper floor of the market building which is beaten when the market is open and closed every day.

- 市楼画像砖（东汉）

此画像砖出土于四川广汉市周村。砖宽48.4厘米，高27厘米，整个画面反映出汉代市场交易繁忙兴旺的情景，是汉代繁盛的商业活动的写照。

Portrayal Brick of Market Building (Eastern Han Dynasty, 25-220)

Unearthed from the Zhoucun Village located in Guanghan City, Sichuan Province, this 48.4-cm-wide and 27-cm-high portrayal brick illustrates the busy and thriving scenes of transactions in the markets of the Han Dynasty (206 B.C.-220 A.D.). It summarizes the prosperous commercial activities in the Han Dynasty.

四川的画像砖

汉代画像砖分布地区较广，但以四川、河南、陕西、山西等省份出土的最多。其中最有特色的要数四川出土的画像砖。四川画像砖以实心砖为主，一般为一砖一画，主题较为独立、完整，画面结构完整有序，题材丰富多样，从各个方面反映了四川地区经济社会的富庶和社会生活的丰富多彩，如宴乐舞戏、庭院楼阙、市井庄园、采桑渔猎、播种收割等。这些以生产劳动和日常生活为题材的画像砖是当时四川人民生活最真实的反映。

Portrayal Bricks from Sichuan Province

Portrayal bricks of the Han Dynasty (206 B.C.-220 A.D.) were widely distributed, but most of them were excavated from Sichuan, Henan, Shaanxi and Shanxi provinces. Among them, the most distinctive ones were unearthed in Sichuan Province. Portrayal bricks from Sichuan Province are mostly solid bricks. By and large, each brick shows a picture with a complete and independent theme. The composition of the picture is neat and structurally complete. There are various subject matters for the portrayal bricks, which reflect the affluent economy and colorful social life in the Sichuan region in different aspects. This includes banquet dances, courtyard and houses, the marketplace and manor, mulberry collecting, fishing and hunting, sowing and harvesting and so on. These portrayal bricks with themes that reflect production labors and daily lives provide a true picture of people's everyday life in Sichuan Province at that time.

• 馈赂画像砖（东汉）（图片提供：FOTOE）
馈赂，带有赠送财物和行贿的意思。

Portrayal Brick of Gift-giving (Eastern Han Dynasty, 25-220)
Gift-giving usually suggests giving gifts or briberies.

- 单阙画像砖拓片（东汉）

汉阙是汉代的一种纪念性建筑，主要指建在城门或建筑群大门外表示威仪等的建筑物。此画像砖在成都郊区出土，正面浮雕一两层单阙，阙顶左右对称，比例恰当，阙两旁各有一人躬身而立，上檐两旁各悬一玩戏小猴，它们为迎谒场面增添了情趣。

The Rubbing of Portrayal Brick of a Single *Que*-tower (Eastern Han Dynasty, 25-220)

The *Que*-tower from the Han Dynasty is a monumental piece of architecture established primarily outside the city gate or the gate of a group of buildings to symbolize the eminence or status involved. This portrayal brick was excavated from the suburbs of Chengdu. Its front surface shows a single *Que*-tower in relief with bilaterally symmetrical and well proportioned overlaid *Que*-tower roofs. There's a person bowing on either side of the tower with a little playful monkey hanging on either side of the top eaves, adding some fun and delight to the welcome scene.

- 百鸟朝凤画像砖（南朝）

凤凰是中国古代传说中的百鸟之王，常用来象征祥瑞。此画像砖上的凤凰展开双翅，似乎正要翩翩起舞，众鸟以凤凰为中心，姿态恭敬。

Portrayal Brick of a Phoenix Worshiped by Hundreds of Birds (Southern Dynasties, 420-589)

The phoenix is the king of all birds in Chinese ancient legend. It is often used to symbolize good omens. The phoenix depicted on this portrayal brick has its wings spread as if it was about to fly. All the birds circle around the phoenix with respectful gestures.

- 车马出行画像砖（东汉）

（图片提供：FOTOE）

此画像砖采用浅浮雕的表现手法，画面生动美观，为研究当时的交通等提供了资料。

Portrayal Brick of the Carriage Tour (Eastern Han Dynasty, 25-220)

This portrayal brick, which reflect how the people of Han used to travel, were crafted using bas-relief techniques. The portrayals are vivid and pretty. They provide information for studying transportation at that time.

076

秦砖汉瓦
Qin Bricks and Han Tiles

- 出行画像砖

  这三块画像砖反映的是南朝时人们出行的情景。

  Portrayal Bricks of Traveling

  All the three portrayal bricks reflect people traveling during the Southern dynasties (420-589).

• 画像砖（汉）
这两块汉砖中人物的动作各不相同，但连在一起便是一幅完整的画面，造型优美，古朴生动。

Portrayal Bricks (Han Dynasty, 206 B.C.-220 A.D.)
The actions of the characters in these two Han bricks are different, but when put together they form a complete picture with beautiful shapes, simplicity and vividness.

• 彩绘画像砖（南朝）

Painted Portrayal Bricks(Southern Dynasties, 420-589)

- **弄玉吹箫图画像砖（南朝）**

此画像砖反映的是一个美好的民间传说。秦国国君秦穆公的女儿弄玉喜爱吹箫，秦穆公疼爱她，便把女儿嫁给了也吹得一手好箫的萧史，并在都城附近建了一座高台，让萧史、弄玉夫妇居住。弄玉和萧史天天练习吹箫，吹出的箫声如同凤鸣。一天，优美的箫声引来一龙一凤，萧史乘龙，弄玉乘凤，双双飞入云霄，升天而去。

Portrayal Brick of Nongyu Playing the Flute (Southern Dynasties, 420-589)

This portrayal brick illustrates a beautiful folklore. Nongyu, the daughter of the Duke Mu of Qin, liked playing flute. The Duke Mu of Qin was so fond of his daughter that he married her to Xiao Shi, a flute expert, and built a high platform in the neighborhood of the capital for the couple to live in. Xiao Shi and Nongyu practiced the flute day by day. The sound of the flute was like the cry of a phoenix. One day, the beautiful sound of their flutes drew forth a loong and a phoenix. Xiao Shi then rode on the loong while Nongyu rode on the phoenix and flew into the clouds.

- 贵妇出游画像砖（南朝）

此砖出土于河南邓县一座南朝墓葬内，描绘了贵族妇女盛装出游的情景。无论贵妇还是丫鬟都身材修长，上束高高的发髻，着宽大裙服，衣带飘飘，婀娜多姿，生动地再现了当时妇女以"广袖高髻"为时尚的社会风气，具有鲜明的时代特征。

Portrayal Brick of Traveling Noblewomen (Southern Dynasties, 420-589)

Unearthed in a tomb of the Southern dynasties (420-589) located in Dengxian County, Henan Province, this portrayal brick depicts a scene of traveling noblewomen. Both the noblewomen and their maidservants are slim in stature, with tall hair buns. Dressed in loose and wide dresses with fluttering belts and bands, they show the feminine grace and typical female fashion styles of wide sleeves and high hair buns at that time, imparting distinctive characteristics of that time.

- 武士画像砖（宋）

武士头戴将军盔，眉头紧锁，怒目圆睁，连腮胡飘于胸前，肩臂饰铠甲，胸铠上系丝带，腰带下的战裙飘垂于膝后，足下蹬战靴，右手持宝剑，正气凛然。

Portrayal Brick of a Warrior (Song Dynasty, 960-1279)

The warrior is wearing a general's helmet, shown in a profile with locked frown and an angry-looking stare, long whiskers flowing in front of his chest. His shoulders are decorated with an armor and a ribbon is tied on the breastplate. His battledress floats around his knees just under the belt. He is wearing battle boots on both feet and wields a sword in his right hand righteousness showing a sense of.

- 烹茶画像砖拓片（宋）（图片提供：FOTOE）

长方形的画像砖。一个少女微微弯着腰，左手下垂，右手执火箸夹拨炉中的炭火。她正在烹茶。这幅画表现了宋代人的饮茶习俗。

The Rubbing of Portrayal Brick of Tea Boiling (Song Dynasty, 960-1279)

This is a rectangular portrayal brick. A young girl is slightly bent over with her left hand drooping and her right hand holding a clamp to kindle the fire in the furnace as she's boiling tea. It illustrates the tea-drinking customs of the Song Dynasty.

• 人物画像砖（北宋）
Portrayal Bricks of Figures (Northern Song Dynasty, 960-1127)

• 西藏画像砖
Xizang Portrayal Brick

• 西藏佛寺砖
The Xizang Buddhist Temple Brick

- **狩猎图画像砖（魏晋）** （图片提供：FOTOE）

  魏晋时期，中国的绘画艺术逐步走向了成熟。此砖画仅寥寥数笔，就将一场狩猎表现得惟妙惟肖。

  Mural Portrayal Brick of Hunting (Wei and Jin Dynasties, 220-420)

  Chinese painting art gradually became mature in the Wei and Jin dynasties. This brick is able to vividly illustrate the scene of a hunt with only a few strokes.

- **采桑及护桑彩绘砖（魏晋）** （图片提供：FOTOE）

  彩绘砖兴起于西汉，终于北宋。彩绘砖仅为富贵之家的墓室、家庙、祠堂所用。

  Color-painted Brick of Collecting Mulberry and Protecting Mulberry (Wei and Jin Dynasties, 220-420)

  Colored-painted bricks originated in the Western Han Dynasty (206 B.C.-25 A.D.), and ended in the Northern Song Dynasty (960-1127). They were used only in the tombs, family temples and ancestral temples of wealthy families.

砖雕

　　砖雕是一种中国传统雕刻艺术，由瓦当、空心砖和汉画像砖等发展而来。砖雕主要以青砖为材料雕刻出山水、花卉、人物以及民居等画面，主要用来装饰民居及寺庙等的构件与墙面，是中国古建筑雕刻中很重要的一种艺术形式。砖雕与木雕、石雕合称为"建筑三雕"。砖雕在北宋时期开始形成并逐渐兴盛，最初主要用来装饰墓室壁面。墓室内的砖雕数量、质量以及所选用的题材，都取决于墓室主人的社会地位。北宋常见的砖雕题材有墓室主人夫妇对坐、男仆托盘和侍女执壶等。金代，墓室砖雕的内容更加丰富，技艺也有所提高。从元代开始，墓室砖雕走向衰落。明代砖雕开始由墓室装饰发展为建筑装饰材料，明代以后的砖雕大多是皇家、官吏、富豪以及地主们宅院的厅堂、大门、照壁、祠堂、戏台等建筑的重要装饰材料，有的还配以灰泥雕塑或镶嵌瓷片。这些砖雕通常雕刻精美，富贵华丽。清代后期，砖雕趋向繁缛细巧，具有绘画的艺术趣味。

Brick Carving

Brick carving is a traditional Chinese carving art evolving from eaves tiles, hollow bricks and portrayal bricks from the Han Dynasty (206 B.C.-220 A.D.). Brick carving mainly use

• 松柏祥鹿吉鸟砖雕
Brick Carvings of Cypress, Auspicious Deer and Lucky Bird

blue blue bricks as materials to carve out landscapes flowers, figures, civil residential houses and the like. They were mainly used to decorate component parts and walls of residential houses, temples and others. Brick carving is a very important form of art in ancient Chinese architectural carvings. It is collectively referred to, along with wood carving and stone carving, as the "three architectural carvings". Brick carving began to emerge and thrive in the Northern Song Dynasty (960-1127), and were initially used to decorate tomb walls. The quantity, quality and subject matters of the brick carvings used in the tomb chambers were all selected in compliance with the social status of the tomb's owner. The subject matters commonly found on the brick carving from the Northern Song Dynasty include the picture showing the tomb owner sitting beside his wife, male servants holding trays, maids holding pots, and so forth. During the Jin Dynasty (265-420), brick carvings from tomb chambers became richer in contents and much skillfully wrought in craft. In the Yuan Dynasty (1206-1368), the brick carvings from tomb chambers began declining. It was during the Ming Dynasty (1368-1644) that the brick carvings evolved from being used for tomb chambers to being used for building decorations. After the Ming Dynasty, brick carvings became important decorative methods mostly used by imperial families, officials, the rich, as well as landlords for the halls or main entrances of their house buildings, and for screen walls, ancestral temples and opera stages. Some of the brick carvings were foiled with plaster sculptures or engraved with ceramic tiles. They were exquisitely carved with elegance and beauty. In the late Qing Dynasty, brick carvings became over-elaborate in details and oriented towards the artistic taste of paintings.

- 麒麟砖雕
Kylin Brick Carving

- 人物砖雕

砖雕大多作为建筑构件或大门、照壁、墙面的装饰。在题材上，砖雕以龙凤呈祥、麒麟送子、狮子滚绣球、松柏、兰花、竹、山茶、菊花、荷花、鲤鱼等寓意吉祥和人们喜闻乐见的内容为主。

Brick Carving with Patterns of Characters

Brick carving are mostly used as building components or decorations of doors, screens and walls. In the subject, loong and phoenix, kylin, lion, pine, orchid, bamboo, chrysanthemum, lotus, camellia, carp and other auspicious pattens are common.

● 砖雕影壁
Screen Wall with Brick Carvings

087 砖 Bricks

● 砖雕门楼
Gatehouse with Brick Carvings

瓦当
Eaves Tiles

　　瓦当也是中国建筑的重要构件之一。瓦当的使用不仅解决了建筑的防水问题，延长了房屋的寿命，而且美化了建筑，其上的纹饰与文字更蕴含了大量的历史文化信息。

The eaves tile is another important element in Chinese architecture. The use of eaves tiles not only solves the waterproofing issue in buildings, but also extends the lifespan of houses and beautifies the architecture. Moreover, the decorative patterns and texts on eaves tiles also bear a vast amount of historical and cultural information.

瓦当按纹饰大致可分三类：一为素面瓦当，二为图案瓦当，三为文字瓦当。如按形状分，还可分为半圆瓦当、大半圆瓦当和圆形瓦当。瓦当质地一般为泥质灰陶，用土色纯黄、黏性较好、沙粒较少的黄壤土烧制而成，个别由砖、石雕刻而成。另外还有铁、铜、鎏金、琉璃的瓦当。瓦当产地范围颇广，陕西、河南等都是著名的瓦当产地。

瓦当的装饰题材广泛，如自然、神话、图腾、历史、民俗、吉语、姓氏等等，融合了书法、绘画、雕塑等多门类艺术，是古代政治、经济、文化的重要信息载体。

Based on the decorative patterns, eaves tiles can be roughly classified into plain-surface eaves tiles, patterned eaves tiles and inscription eaves tiles. They can also be divided by shape into the semi-cylindrical eaves tiles, three-quarter cylindrical eaves tiles, and cylindrical eaves tiles. The usual material of eaves tiles is the argillaceous grey pottery burnt out of the yellowish soil with good viscosity and little sand. Some of them are carved from bricks or stones. There are also eaves tiles made of cast iron, copper, gold gilt and glass. Eaves tiles have a vast range of production locations. Provinces including Shaanxi and Henan were well-known production centers for eaves tiles.

There is a wide range of decorative

大半圆瓦当（秦）(图片提供: FOTOE)

大半圆瓦当是为保护建筑物顶部的檩子特制的。由于这种瓦当非常大，不像一般瓦当用于椽头，而是用于檩头，既起装饰作用，又防檩子腐烂，因此又名"遮朽"。制作时，切去圆形筒瓦底部的约1/4即可，直径一般为50—70厘米。图中瓦当上有山状的变形夔纹。这种大半圆瓦当安装在皇家宫殿的檩头上，流行于秦代。

Three-quarter Cylindrical Eaves Tiles (Qin Dynasty, 221 B.C.-206 B.C.)

Three-quarter cylindrical eaves tiles were specifically designed to protect the purlin on roofs of buildings. Due to their large size, such eaves tiles were not used at the top of rafters like ordinary eaves tiles, but at the top of the purlin. Since it can be used to decorate and prevent the purlin from rotting, it is also known as the "rot-cover". To produce it, a cylindrical eaves tile with a diameter of approximately 50 to 70 cm has a quarter cut off. The surface of this eaves tiles was decorated with morphed *Kui*-loong patterns in the shape of a mountain. This type of three-quarter cylindrical eaves tile was usually installed on both ends of the purlin in the imperial palaces and was popular during the Qin Dynasty.

重环纹半瓦当（西周）

重环纹是由若干个近椭圆形的环组成的纹样。重环纹半瓦当均出土于陕西扶风西周时期的建筑遗址，多为泥质灰陶或泥质红陶，直径一般为17—25.2厘米。重环纹瓦当图案沿袭了西周青铜器纹饰风格，这种风格一直被沿用到秦代。

Semi-cylindrical Eaves Tile with Double-ring Patterns (Western Zhou Dynasty, 1046 B.C.-771 B.C.)

The double-ring pattern is composed of oval-shaped rings. Semi-cylindrical eaves tiles with double-ring patterns were all unearthed in the architectural ruins from the Western Zhou Dynasty in Fufeng, Shaanxi Province. They are mostly made of argillaceous grey pottery or argillaceous red pottery, with diameters usually ranging from 17 to 25.2 cm. The double-ring patterns of the eaves tiles were borrowed from the bronze ware of the Western Zhou Dynasty. This decoration style was used to the Qin Dynasty (221 B.C.-206 B.C.).

themes for eaves tiles, such as nature, mythologies, totems, histories, folklore, auspicious words, family names, etc. They combine the art of calligraphy, painting, sculpture and many other categories of craft. Eaves tiles are important information carriers of ancient politics, economics and cultures.

- 太阳纹半瓦当（春秋）

Sun-patterned Semi-cylindrical Eaves Tile (Spring and Autumn Period, 770 B.C.-476 B.C.)

- 燕国人面半瓦当（战国）

Human Face-patterned Semi-cylindrical Eaves Tile of the Yan State (Warring States Period, 475 B.C.-221 B.C.)

- 燕国双龙纹半瓦当（战国）

Two Loongs-patterned Semi-cylindrical Eaves Tile of the Yan State (Warring States Period, 475 B.C.-221 B.C.)

> 素面瓦当

素面瓦当的当面不饰任何纹饰，一般为半圆瓦当，少数为圆形瓦当。素面半圆瓦当盛行于春秋中晚期至战国早期，在陕西扶风和岐山西周遗址、河南洛阳东周王城遗址、河北邯郸赵都遗址、陕西凤翔秦雍城遗址、陕西咸阳秦咸阳城遗址等均有出土。秦汉时期素面瓦当逐渐减少。

> Plain-surface Eaves Tiles

The plain-surface eaves tile has an undecorated surface. Most of them are semi-cylindrical in shape, although a few of them are full cylindrical. Plain-surface semi-cylindrical eaves tiles were prevalent from the mid-and-late Spring and Autumn Period to the early Warring States Period. They were excavated from the ruins of the Western Zhou Dynasty located in Fufeng and Qishan, in Shaanxi Province, the ruins of the imperial city of the Eastern Zhou Dynasty in Luoyang, Henan Province, the ruins of capital of the Zhao State in Handan, Hebei Province,

• 素面瓦当（西周）
Plain-surface Eaves Tile (Western Zhou Dynasty, 1046 B.C.-771 B.C.)

• 袁耀《阿房宫图》（清）

阿房宫是秦始皇统一六国后修筑的豪华宫殿。阿房宫位于秦都咸阳上林苑内。史书记载，秦始皇曾征集上百万人修筑秦始皇陵和阿房宫。

Painting of the Epang Palace by Yuanyao (Qing Dynasty, 1616-1911)

Epang Palace is a luxurious palace built within the Shanglin Garden in Xianyang, capital of Qin, after the First Emperor of Qin unified the Six States. According to the history books, the first emperor of Qin recruited and gathered millions of people to construct the Mausoleum of the First Emperor of Qin and the Epang Palace.

• 素面鱼形瓦当（明）

Plain-surface Eaves Tile in Fish-shaped (Ming Dynasty, 1368-1644)

the ruins of Yongcheng City of the Qin Dynasty (221-206 B.C.) in Fengxiang, Shaanxi Province, and the ruins of Xianyang City of the Qin Dynasty. Plain-surface eaves tiles gradually dwindled during the Qin and Han dynasties (221 B.C.-220 A.D.).

> 图案瓦当

　　图案瓦当上的纹饰一般有动物纹、植物纹和云纹三种。

　　早期瓦当动物纹为单一动物，如鹿、鸟、獾、夔、虎、豹、蟾蜍等；中期为对称的扇面状，每个扇面上都有双兽、禽鸟和人物等。

　　秦代的动物纹图案瓦当最多，纹样有鹿纹、夔龙纹、夔凤纹、豹纹、鱼纹等。这些瓦当上的图案以

> Patterned Eaves Tiles

Patterned eaves tiles are generally decorated with patterns of animals, plants or clouds.

　　Early animal patterns of patterned eaves tiles were composed of single animals, such as the deer, bird, badger, *Kui* (a one-legged monster in fable), tiger, leopard, toad, etc. During its mid-phase, the patterned eaves tiles were symmetrical fan-shaped with paired

- **夔龙纹瓦当（秦）**

夔又称"夔牛"，是传说中的一种怪兽，外形似龙，声音如雷，仅有一足。古人认为夔能辟邪。这件瓦当上的夔龙造型简单，线条古朴，以直线线条组合构成夔龙形象。

***Kui*-loong-patterned Eaves Tile (Qin Dynasty, 221 B.C.-206 B.C.)**

Kui, also known as *Kuiniu*, is a legendary loong-shaped monster with a thunder-like voice and only one foot. People in ancient China believed the *Kui* was able to ward off evil. The *Kui*-loong on this eaves tile is simplistic in design, using quaint outlines and straight lines to form the *Kui*-loong pattern.

谐音的手法寓意吉祥，反映了秦人祈福求吉的心理，如貛寓"欢"，鹿寓"禄"，鱼寓"余"等，这为后代吉祥图案的流行开了先河。

汉代时动物纹瓦当越来越少，最常见的"四神瓦当"多出土于汉长安城等宫殿建筑遗址。四神瓦当十分注意细部的刻画，如青龙的鳞甲、朱雀的羽毛、玄武的龟纹等。

- 鹿纹瓦当（秦）
此瓦当仅以一只奔跑的鹿覆盖全部画面，虽然简单，却显得简约秀美。

Deer-patterned Eaves Tile (Qin Dynasty, 221 B.C.-206 B.C.)

This eaves tile features nothing but a running deer over the entire surface. Although simple, it looks concise and pretty.

animals, birds or figures patterns.

Among animal-patterned eaves tiles, the most are from the Qin Dynasty (221 B.C.-206 B.C.). The patterns included deer, *Kui*-loong, *Kui*-phoenix, leopard, fish and the like. The patterns of these eaves tiles played on homophonic words to denote good luck, which reflected the psychology of the Qin people in their prayers for good fortune. For instance, badger (*Huan* in Chinese) stands for joy (also *Huan* in Chinese), deer (*Lu* in Chinese) stands for wealth (also *Lu* in Chinese), and fish (*Yu* in Chinese) for more or surplus (also *Yu* in Chinese). This paved the way for the auspicious patterns in later generations.

Although animal-patterned eaves tiles dwindled during the Han Dynasty (206 B.C.-220 A.D.), Eaves Tiles of Four Sacred Animals, however, became pervasive. They were mostly excavated from the architectural relic sites of palaces in Chang'an City or elsewhere from the Han Dynasty. Great attention was given to details of the carved patterns on the Eaves Tiles of Four Sacred Animals, such as the distinctive scales of the loong,

- 豹纹瓦当

豹为食肉兽，性格凶猛。此瓦中豹四肢强健，形态彪悍，奔跑之中回首怒吼。豹身的金钱花纹美轮美奂，突出于当面。在两千多年前，瓦当的制作工艺就已经达到了极高的水平。

Leopard-patterned Eaves Tile

Leopards are carnivorous animals, ferocious in nature. The leopard portrayed on this eaves tile has strong limbs and sturdy body shape. It is roaring while looking back on the run. The body of the leopard is fully covered with gorgeous dot patterns that bulge out of the surface. The manufacturing techniques for eaves tiles had reached a high level 2,000 years ago.

四神纹瓦当分置于殿阁东、西、南、北四个不同的方位上，寓意辟邪镇宅，保佑社稷长存，江山永固。四神纹样有多种样式，直到今天仍被广泛用于装饰图案中。而狮子纹瓦当则流行于隋唐。

植物纹瓦当的出现略晚于动物

feathers of the sparrow, and the moire on the black tortoise, which is meant to ward off evil from the house, protect the family and bless the country and its territory with everlasting well-being. There have been a great variety of Four Sacred Animals patterns, and they are still widely used to date as decorative patterns. Lion-patterned eaves tiles became popular in the Sui and Tang dynasties (581-907).

Vegetation-patterned eaves tiles emerged later than the animal-patterned ones, during the mid-to-late Warring States Period. The vegetation-patterned eaves tiles had their surface decorated with pictures of plants. They were mostly cylindrical in shape, with only a few of them being semi-cylindrical. Their patterns were mostly leaves, sunflower petals, lotus petals etc. Vegetation-patterned eaves tiles were excavated from the ruins of such ancient cities of Qin as Yongcheng, Zhiyang and Xianyang. The most famous among them were the eaves tiles with patterns of lotus flowers unearthed from the ruins of Yongcheng City and the Epang Palace relics. Due to the influence of Buddhism, eaves tiles patterned with lotus flowers became popularized from the Northern Wei Dynasty (386-534).

• 奔虎瓦当（战国）

奔虎造型生动，虎口大张，作飞跑回首状，展现了虎的威猛神态。在中国古代，虎是勇猛威武的象征。

Eaves Tile with Patterns of a Running Tiger (Warring States Period, 475 B.C.-221 B.C.)

The running tiger is rendered in a vivid style with its mouth wide open and is looking back while running. The mighty demeanor of a tiger is fully illustrated. In ancient China, the tiger is a symbol of bravery and might.

• 双獾瓦当（战国）

此瓦当中两獾相对，颈部相交，竖耳张口，卷尾利爪，头似前伸，又似回顾，构思奇特生动，形象逼真。

Eaves Tile with Patterns of Two Badgers (Warring States Period, 475 B.C.-221 B.C.)

The two badgers on this eaves tile are facing each other with their necks joined together, ears up, mouths open, tails curled, sharp claws exposed and heads leaning forward while their eyes are looking back. With its extraordinary composition, this picture is strangely vivid and lifelike.

• 四鹤半瓦当（战国）

Semi-cylindrical Eaves Tile with Patterns of Four Cranes (Warring States Period, 475 B.C-221 B.C.)

• 虎逐鹿瓦当（战国）

Eaves Tile with Patterns of a Tiger Chasing a Deer (Warring States Period, 475 B.C.-221 B.C.)

• 燕国饕餮纹半瓦当（战国）

（图片提供：FOTOE）

Taotie-patterned Semi-cylindrical Eaves Tile of the Yan State (Warring States Period, 475 B.C.-221 B.C.)

• 燕国兽面纹半瓦当（战国）

（图片提供：FOTOE）

The Semi-cylindrical Eaves Tile with Beast Face Pattern of the Yan State (Warring States Period, 475 B.C.-221 B.C.)

• 燕国兽面纹半瓦当（战国）

（图片提供：FOTOE）

The Semi-cylindrical Eaves Tile with Beast Face Pattern of the Yan State (Warring States Period, 475 B.C.-221 B.C.)

• 兽面纹琉璃瓦当（西夏）

Glazed Eaves Tile with Patterns of Animal Face (Western Xia Dynasty, 1038-1227)

- 金乌纹瓦当（汉）

  金乌是古代先民用来代表太阳的图腾。金乌瓦当一般瓦体硕大，造型奇异。这件瓦当是汉武帝甘泉宫建筑的重要构件。甘泉宫是汉代最重要的宫殿之一，汉武帝在此接见诸侯王，宴请客宾，并用作避暑离宫。

  Eaves Tile with Patterns of Golden Bird (Han Dynasty, 206 B.C.-220 A.D.)

  The golden bird is a totem used by ancient people to symbolize the sun. The eaves tile with patterns of golden birds usually has a sizable body and outstanding shape. This tile was an important component used in the construction of Emperor Wu of Han's Ganquan Palace. Ganquan Palace is the most important palace of the Han Dynasty (206 B.C.-220 A.D.), where Emperor Wu of Han held meetings with feudal lords, hosted banquets and feasts for guests and lived during the summer.

- 曲龙纹瓦当（汉）

  在中国古代的神话传说中，龙是能兴云作雨的神异动物。封建时代龙还是皇权的象征，皇帝称为真龙天子，皇室用物也多用龙装饰。

  Eaves Tile with Patterns of Curved Loong (Han Dynasty, 206 B.C.-220 A.D.)

  In Chinese myths and legends, the loong is a mystical animal that can summon up wind and rain. During the feudal ages, loongs served as the symbol of the imperial power. The emperor was called the real son of the loong and most items used in the imperial family were decorated with images of the loong.

四象

　　四象依次为青龙、白虎、朱雀、玄武，象征东、西、南、北，它们是以自然界的动物为原形加以想象而被创造出来的。青龙象征东方、左方、春天；白虎象征西方、右方、秋天；朱雀是理想中的吉鸟，象征南方、下方、夏天；玄武是由龟和蛇组合而成的，象征北方、上方、冬天。四象也是四种颜色的象征，即蓝（青龙）、白（白虎）、红（朱雀）、黑（玄武）。

Four Symbols

The Four Symbols, the azure loong, white tiger, red sparrow and black tortoise, are four divine animals that symbolize the east, west, south, and north respectively. These divine animals were created on the basis of real animals in nature, coupled with a tint of imagination. Among the Four Symbols, the azure loong stands for the east, left side and the season of spring. It is the leader of the Four Symbols. The white tiger symbolizes the west, right side and autumn. The red sparrow, an idealistic auspicious bird, indicates the south, down side, and summer. The black tortoise is a combination of the tortoise and the snake, which symbolizes the north, upper side, and winter. The Four Symbols also stand for four colors, the azure loong for blue, white tiger for white, the red sparrow for red and the black tortoise for black.

- **青龙瓦当（汉）**

此瓦当为圆形，边廓较宽，略有残损。瓦当上的青龙躯体强健，颈、腹下有鳞甲，肋间生翅，背部有表示东方初升太阳的图案，形象洒脱奔放，活灵活现，极为勇武。这件瓦当做工细腻，鳞甲刻画清晰，布局充实丰满，是汉代图案瓦当中的精品。

Eaves Tile with Patterns of Azure Loong (Han Dynasty, 206 B.C.-220 A.D.)

Cylindrical in shape, this eaves tile has a wide-edged profile, slightly damaged. The azure loong on the eaves tile is robust, with scales on its neck and belly, wings and a sign of the sun on its back to indicate the rising sun from the east. The image is lively, imaginative, vivid and extremely chivalrous. The craftsmanship is delicate, the scales are distinctive and the layout is full and complete, all of which makes it a masterpiece among the eaves tiles from the Han Dynasty (206 B.C.-220 A.D.).

- 白虎瓦当（汉）

此瓦当中白虎依托圆瓦而呈弧形，动感强烈，蕴含气势，突出了老虎的威严，老虎背部有落日。

Eaves Tile with Patterns of White Tiger (Han Dynasty, 206 B.C.-220 A.D.)

The white tiger depicted on this eaves tile relies on the circular tile to highlight its curved shape in strong dynamics and is full of momentum, showing the majesty of a tiger. A setting sun is shown behind the tiger.

- 朱雀瓦当（汉）

此瓦当图案中，朱雀为凤头、鹰喙、鸾颈、鱼尾，可见朱雀是人们想象出来的神鸟。

Eaves Tile with Patterns of Red Sparrow (Han Dynasty, 206 B.C.-220 A.D.)

In the eaves tile, the red sparrow is shown with the head of a phoenix, the beak of an eagle, the neck of a *Luan* (a mythical bird-like phoenix) and the tail of a fish. It is clear that the red sparrow is a divine creature created by the people.

- 玄武瓦当（汉）

此瓦当为龟蛇纹。一龟头部高昂，龟身和足压在蛇身上；蛇首对龟怒目张口，蛇身沿瓦当边沿和龟身缠绕。龟身饰"井"字形纹，蛇身饰鳞纹。

Eaves Tile with Patterns of Black Tortoise (Han Dynasty, 206 B.C.-220 A.D.)

This is a pattern of a tortoise and a snake, with the head of the tortoise held high and its body and tail on top of the snake body. The snake's mouth is angrily opened toward the tortoise, while its body is tightly wrapped around the tortoise body. The tortoise's shell is decorated with patterns of the Chinese character "井" and the snake's body is decorated with scale patterns.

- 飞凤纹瓦当（明）
  Eaves Tile with Flying Phoenix Pattern
  (Ming Dynasty, 1368-1644)

- 瓦当（辽）
  Eaves Tile (Liao Dynasty, 907-1125)

- 飞天瓦当（唐）
  Flying Apsaras-patterned Eaves Tile
  (Tang Dynasty, 618-907)

- 奔貛瓦当（战国）

  Eaves Tile with Pattern of a Running Badger (Warring States Period, 475 B.C.-221 B.C.)

- 灵寿古城建筑瓦当（战国）

  Architectural Tile of Lingshou Old Town (Warring States Period, 475 B.C.-221 B.C.)

- 蟾蜍瓦当（战国）

  Eaves Tile with Pattern of a Toad (Warring States Period, 475 B.C.-221 B.C.)

纹瓦当，大约出现于战国中晚期。植物纹瓦当的当面饰有植物纹，大部分瓦当为圆形，少数为半圆形，纹饰以树叶、葵瓣、莲瓣等居多。秦代植物纹瓦当在秦故都雍城、芷阳、咸阳等地均有出土，以雍城和阿房宫遗址出土的莲花纹瓦当最著名。从北魏开始，因受佛教的影响，以莲花为主图案的瓦当开始盛行。

云纹瓦当同样大部分为圆瓦当。云纹图案在其发展演变过程中吸收了自然界中的云朵、花枝、羊角、蘑菇等形象，逐渐形成了较为抽象的卷云纹图案。从十六国到北朝，瓦当的云纹趋于简化并逐渐消失。

Likewise, cloud-patterned eaves tiles were mostly cylindrical in shape. During its development and evolution, cloud-patterned eaves tiles absorbed such elements in nature as clouds, flowered twigs, goat horns, mushrooms and more and eventually brought in the abstract patterns of cirrus clouds. From the Sixteen States Period (304-439) to the Northern dynasties (386-581), the cloud patterns on eaves tiles became simplified and gradually disappeared.

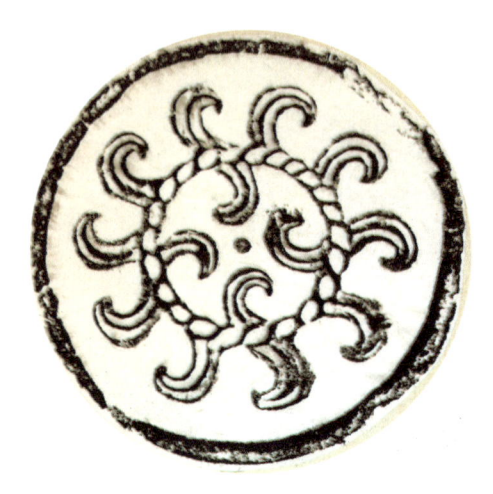

- 莲纹瓦当拓片（秦）

此瓦当中心有一圆钮，外围为同心圆，瓦当边框与同心圆之间有纵横的莲花瓣，图案古朴、和谐、美观，是典型的植物纹瓦当。秦代瓦当上的莲花图案与佛教传入中国后出现的莲花图案是有区别的。

The Rubbing of Lotus-patterned Eaves Tile (Qin Dynasty, 221 B.C.-206 B.C.)

There is a round button in the center of this eaves tile, surrounded by concentric circles. Lotus petals can be found on the border and concentric circles of the eaves tile. The picture is simple, harmonious and beautiful. It is a classic example of vegetation-patterned eaves tiles. The lotus patterns on eaves tiles of the Qin Dynasty vary from those after the introduction of Buddhism into China.

- 葵纹瓦当（战国）

战国初期，葵纹瓦当出现并很快流行起来。葵纹瓦当装饰性强，品种繁多，成为秦瓦当的大宗。早期饰以辐射纹，并在辐射纹周围加以卷曲的水波纹或"S"纹，以单线为主；中期发展为双线，中心圆和外围的区别较大，葵瓣较为粗壮，弯曲度较大，葵瓣切入中心圆，浑然一体。这些葵纹华丽美观，富有韵律感。葵纹后来逐渐向云纹过渡，西汉初年被云纹取代。

Sunflower-patterned Eaves Tile (Warring States Period, 475 B.C.-221 B.C.)

Sunflower-patterned eaves tiles appeared and caught on quickly during the early Warring States Period. The highly decorative sunflower patterns came in vast varieties and became the most typical pattern of eaves tiles in the Qin Dynasty. Early sunflower-patterned eaves tiles were decorated with radiation patterns enclosed in patterns of curved water ripple or "S" patterns, all traced with singular lines. However, during its middle phase, there developed the double-line sunflower patterns with sharp differences between the circles in the center and those in the outer rings. The sunflower petals looked bigger and tougher, more curved and were present in the circles in the center to form an integral whole. These sunflower-patterned eaves tiles were gorgeous and beautiful, loaded with a rich sense of rhythm. Sunflower-patterned gradually shifted to the cloud-patterned and were eventually replaced by the cloud patterns in the early Western Han Dynasty.

- 葵纹瓦当拓片

The Rubbing of Sunflower-patterned Eaves Tile

• 水涡纹瓦当拓片（战国）

水涡纹是古代青铜器纹饰中常见的一种，顾名思义，纹样形似水涡，故名水涡纹。其特征为中间为一圆圈，做水涡激起状。这种纹饰盛行于商周时期。

The Rubbing of Ripple-patterned Eaves Tile (Warring States Period, 475 B.C.-221 B.C.)

The ripple pattern was very common on ancient bronze ware. As its name implies, the pattern bears a similarity to water ripples. It features a circle in the center serving as the center of the roused water surface. The pattern prevailed in the Shang and Zhou dynasties (1600 B.C.-256 B.C.).

• 卷云纹瓦当（秦）

云纹瓦当样式极为丰富，变化多种多样，在秦旧都雍城、栎阳和秦都咸阳三处遗址出土最多。

Eaves Tile with Patterns of Curled Clouds (Qin Dynasty, 221 B.C.-206 B.C.)

Cloud-patterned eaves tiles were extremely rich in variety. Most of them were excavated from the ruins of Yongcheng, Yueyang, and Xianyang from the Qin Dynasty.

- 兽面纹琉璃瓦当
  Glazed Eaves Tiles with Face of Beast

- 黄琉璃龙纹瓦当
  龙首居中，龙身随瓦当舒展，显得美观大方。
  Yellow Glazed Eaves Tile with Loong Pattern
  The loong head is located in the center. The body of the loong stretches with the tile and looks beautiful and graceful.

• 人面瓦当（北朝）

人面瓦当是瓦当纹饰中的罕见品种。"人面"是其最重要的特征，除了用线条表现外，鼻、眼、面多用块状造型来描绘。这类瓦当给人一种全新的视觉感受。

Eaves Tiles with Patterns of a Human Face (Northern Dynasties, 386-581)

The eaves tile with pattern of a human face is a very rare type of patterned eaves tile. The "human face" is its most important feature. In addition to lines, the nose, eyes and the face contour are mostly portrayed with block shapes. This type of pattern offers a new kind of visual experience.

• 莲花纹瓦当（唐）

这是三种风格略微不同的莲花纹瓦当，它们纹饰均简洁流畅，轻盈飘逸，体现了隋唐莲花纹瓦当自然古朴的风格。

Eaves Tiles with Patterns of Lotus Flowers (Tang Dynasty, 618-907)

These are three patterned eaves tiles with slightly different types of lotus flowers. With clear and fluent depictions, the lotus flowers are graced with light and elegant grains, which reflects the natural and quaint style of the lotus flower patterns on the eaves tiles from the Sui and Tang dynasties (581-907).

• 狮子纹瓦当（唐）
Lion-patterned Eaves Tile (Tang Dynasty, 618-907)

• 泉州学馆瓦当（唐）
这是一件琉璃制瓦当，虽然制作不是很精细，但表明琉璃瓦当在唐代时已经出现。

Eaves Tile of the Ancient School of Quanzhou Area (Tang Dynasty, 618-907)

Although it is made of colored glaze without much sophistication, this eaves tile indicates that glazed eaves tiles had appeared in the Tang Dynasty (618-907).

- 龙纹瓦当（明）
  Loong-patterned Eaves Tile (Ming Dynasty, 1368-1644)

- 龙纹瓦当（清）
  Loong-patterned Eaves Tile (Qing Dynasty, 1616-1911)

瓦当
Eaves Tiles

> ## 文字瓦当

瓦当上所饰文字，很多直接反映了制作时人们的愿望和追求，因此文字瓦当不仅是一种建筑装饰材料，更是历史信息的载体。在考古界，有秦汉文字的瓦当还是宫殿及其他建筑物为秦汉时期建筑的标识。这主要是因为瓦当文字内容以宫殿及其他建筑物名称为主，也有地名、市

> ## Inscription-patterned Eaves Tiles

Most of the Chinese characters decorated on eaves tiles directly reflected the desire and pursuit of the people when they produced them. Therefore, text-patterned eaves tiles are not just architectural decoration materials, but also carriers of historical information. In the archaeological community, eaves

- "卫"字瓦当（秦）

该瓦当出土于阿房宫遗址，当面仅一"卫"字。秦始皇每灭掉一个诸侯国，总要仿建其宫室，"卫"字瓦当是为仿建卫国的宫室而烧制的。

Eaves Tile with Character of *Wei* (Qin Dynasty, 221 B.C.-206 B.C.)

Unearthed from the ruins of the Epang Palace, the surface of this eaves tile was inscribed with the Chinese character *Wei* (卫). For each vassal state eliminated, an imitation of their original palace was built by the first emperor of Qin. The eaves tiles with the character of *Wei* were made as a replica of the palace of the Wei State.

"橐泉宫当"瓦当（汉）

橐泉宫曾是秦雍城的著名宫殿，距离蕲年宫不远，这件汉代的"橐泉宫当"表明橐泉宫在汉代时尚在维修使用，抑或是在原址重建仍袭旧名。

Eaves Tile with Characters of Tuoquan Palace (Han Dynasty, 206 B.C.-220 A.D.)

The Tuoquan Palace in Yongcheng City near the Qinian Palace was a famous palace in the Qin Dynasty (221 B.C.-206 B.C.). This Eaves Tile of Tuoquan Palace from the Han Dynasty implies that the Tuoquan Palace was once repaired or maintained during the Han Dynasty, or that a new construction was built on the same location, carrying on the name of the original palace.

"前堂食事"瓦当（汉）

此瓦当是汉代主管饮食机构的建筑用瓦当。

Eaves Tile with Characters of Front Mess Hall (Han Dynasty, 206 B.C.-220 A.D.)

This eaves tile was used by people in charge of the catering department during the Han Dynasty.

tiles with Chinese characters from the Qin and Han dynasties (221 B.C.-220 A.D.) were considered as signs for the palaces and other architectures from the Qin and Han dynasties. This is because the inscription-patterned eaves tiles excavated mainly bore the names of palaces and other architectures, although some were names of locations, city offices, notes and auspicious words. They are important evidence with which to identify the palaces and other architectures at that time.

Inscription-patterned eaves tiles originated from the Warring States Period (475 B.C.-221 B.C.) and reached a peak during the Han Dynasty (206 B.C.-220 A.D.). They were exquisitely made and the characters on them were elegant, becoming a research category in the field of epigraphy. Based on content, inscription-patterned eaves tiles from the Han Dynasty can be classified into those of palaces, government offices, tombs, ancestral temples, notes and memos, auspicious words and the miscellaneous.

Eaves tiles also provide valuable information for the research of ancient Chinese calligraphy. The characters on eaves tiles were mostly in seal script, although some were in the clerical script or the bird-and-insect scripts (bird-

- **"鼎湖延寿宫"瓦当（汉）**

  鼎湖延寿宫是汉武帝时修建在上林苑最东边的一处离宫。

  Eaves Tile with Characters of Dinghu Longevity Palace (Han Dynasty, 206 B.C.-220 A.D.)

  The Dinghu Longevity Palace was an imperial villa-palace built in the most eastern end of the Shanglin Garden during the Han Dynasty.

- **"上林农官"瓦当（汉）**

  "上林农官"瓦当，即上林苑农事治事处的瓦当。秦汉之际，朝廷采取一系列政治、经济、法律措施确保农业发展，各级官吏以农政为首务，形成举国重农之势。

  Eaves Tile with Characters of Shanglin Agriculture Officer (Han Dynasty, 206 B.C.-220 A.D.)

  The eaves tiles with patterns of Shanglin Agriculture Officer were used by the government office for agriculture officers in Shanglin. During the Qin and Han dynasties (221 B.C.-220A.D.), the governments adopted a series of political, economic and legal measures to ensure the development of agriculture. Officials at all levels set agricultural affairs as their top priority and the whole country attached importance to agriculture.

署、记事和吉语，是识别宫殿建筑年代的重要凭证。

　　文字瓦当起源于战国时代，到了汉代，文字瓦当的发展步入巅峰时期，制作精美、文字隽秀，成为后代金石学的研究内容之一。汉代

and-insect script is a type of text that lies between words and drawings, very similar to artistic words and patterned words). Within limited space, the featured character should conform to the shape of the tiles. Strokes are either long

上林苑

　　上林苑在秦朝时修建，汉武帝时期加以扩建。上林苑地跨西安、咸阳及周边地区，其范围东西长约100公里，南北长约30公里，总面积接近3000平方公里，是中国历史上最大的皇家园林。苑内有极为丰富的自然景物以及大量华美的宫室建筑。

Shanglin Garden

Built during the Qin Dynasty (221 B.C.-206 B.C.), the Shanglin Garden was expanded with new buildings during the reign of Emperor Wu of the Han Dynasty(140 B.C.-87 B.C.). Stretching over Xi'an, Xianyang and the surrounding areas, the Shanglin Garden had an east-to-west span of around 100 km, a north-to-south span of around 30 km with a total area nearing 3,000 km^2, which makes it the largest imperial garden in Chinese history. The garden is rich in natural scenery and comprises a large number of beautiful palace buildings.

- **阿房宫复原图**（图片提供：FOTOE）
  阿房宫是秦上林苑内的建筑之一。
  Restoration of the Epang Palace
  The Epang Palace is one of the buildings in Shanglin Garden.

- "阳陵泾置"瓦当（汉）

此瓦当出土于西汉景帝阳陵邑遗址。"置"为古代传递邮件和迎送宾客的驿站，"泾置"是设在阳陵邑的驿站名。此瓦当的发现为研究西汉帝陵的建制和邮置制度提供了实物依据。

Eaves Tile with Characters of the Yangling Post Station (Han Dynasty, 206 B.C.-220 A.D.)

This eaves tile was unearthed in the ruins of Yangling City of the Emperor Jing of the Western Han Dynasty. The post station (called *Zhi* in Chinese) was an inn for mail delivery and guest reception. The post station (called *Jingzhi* in Chinese) was established in Yangling City. The discovery of this eaves tile has provided physical basis for studying the organization of imperial mausoleums as well as the mail systems in the Western Han Dynasty.

- "八风寿存当"瓦当（汉）

此瓦当是王莽在长安城八风台的用瓦。文字的意思是：天地和合，八风应节，四时有序，万物有成，国运久存，天下康宁。王莽篡权建立新朝（9—23）后，为证明自己是真命天子，修筑了八风台。该瓦当的发现，为研究新莽时期的历史提供了珍贵的实物资料。

Eaves Tile with Characters of Eight-wind Longevity (Han Dynasty, 206 B.C.-220 A.D.)

This eaves tile was used by Wang Mang at the Eight-wind Tower in Chang'an City. The text means: "With Heaven and Earth joined in harmony, four seasons greeted by the winds from eight directions in order and harvest reaped in abundance, the country shall enjoy ever-lasting fate and people of the world shall enjoy health and peace." After he established the Xin Dynasty (9-23), in order to justify himself as the heavenly-approved emperor of China, Wang Mong ordered the construction of the Eight-wind Tower. The discovery of the Eight-wind Longevity eaves tile has provided valuable material for studying the history of the Xin Dynasty.

• 几何纹铭文砖（汉）
Brick with Patterns of the Geometric Pattern and the Inscription (Han Dynasty, 206 B.C.-220 A.D.)

文字瓦当的内容可分为宫殿、官署、陵墓、祠堂、记事、吉语、杂类等。

瓦当还是研究中国古代书法的宝贵资料。瓦当文字多为篆书，也有少见的隶书和鸟虫书（鸟虫书是介于文字与绘画之间的一种书体，接近美术字和图案字）。在这一特定范围内，字体随形就势，笔画或长或短，字形不取方正，充分发挥了篆文书法的装饰艺术效果。据统计，瓦当篆文的变化有120种之多。因内容丰富，书法高妙，备受历代文人墨客推崇。

or short without prescribed upright forms, fully exercising the decorative art effect of the seal-script calligraphy. Statistics have shown that there are as many as 120 variations of the seal script found on the inscription-patterned eaves tiles. Due to their rich content and sublime calligraphy, they were greatly admired by ancient literati and calligraphers.

- **"冢舍"瓦当（汉）**

冢舍瓦，为汉代祠堂、冢墓所用之瓦。当时各家族都有祭祀祖先的祠堂。此瓦当文字优美，存世极罕，所以弥足珍贵。

Eaves Tile of with Characters of Graves (Han Dynasty, 206 B.C.-220 A.D.)

The eaves tiles with characters of graves were used for tombs and ancestral temples of the Han Dynasty. During that time, every family had an ancestral temple where they worshiped their ancestors. The writings on this eaves tile are so elegant that its rarity has made it extremely precious and valuable.

- **"高安万世"瓦当（汉）**

此瓦当多在义陵附近出土。据《汉书》记载，汉哀帝宠臣董贤曾被封为"高安侯"，因此有人认为此瓦当可能为董贤墓的建筑用瓦，也有人推测该瓦当是西汉寺庙的建筑用瓦。

Eaves Tiles of *Gao'an* for Ever (Han Dynasty, 206 B.C.-220 A.D.)

These eaves tiles were mostly discovered in the Yiling Mausoleum of the Western Han Dynasty. According to the *Book of the Han Dynasty*, Emperor Ai's favorite minion, Dong Xian, was dubbed the Marquis of *Gao'an*. Therefore, it is speculated that these eaves tiles may be used for building Dong Xian's tomb, while others believed that they were used to build temples during the Western Han Dynasty.

• "尧舜禹汤"瓦当（汉）

尧、舜、禹、汤是中国古代四位英明的君主。此瓦当是汉代神庙建筑用瓦。

Eaves Tile with Characters of Yao, Shun, Yu and Tang (Han Dynasty, 206 B.C.-220 A.D.)

Yao, Shun, Yu and Tang were four wise monarchs in ancient China. This eaves tile was used for building temples during the Han Dynasty.

• "朝神之宫"瓦当（汉）

Eaves Tile with Characters of God-worshiping Temple (Han Dynasty, 206 B.C.-220 A.D.)

• "京师仓当"瓦当（汉）

瓦当上的文字通常可作为判断古代建筑年代、地址的实证，如该瓦当的出土就指明了西汉京师仓的具体位置。京师仓遗址位于陕西华阴，又名"华仓"，建于汉武帝时期（前140-前87），是为长安贮存、转运粮食的大型粮仓，容量上万立方米。而这样重要的遗址就是靠一块小小的瓦当找到的。京师仓遗址规模大，保存好，是目前发现的规模最大的西汉粮仓建筑遗址，对研究汉代建筑史、经济史、漕渠航运等都具有重要价值。

Eaves Tile with Characters of Capital Granary (Han Dynasty, 206 B.C.-220 A.D.)

Texts inscribed on eaves tiles often serve as evidence in determining the age and location of the ancient architecture involved. For example, the unearthing of this eaves tile indicated the location of the capital granary during the Western Han Dynasty (206 B.C.-25A.D.). The ruins of the capital granary were located in Huayin, Shaanxi Province, also known as Hua Granary. Built in the period of Emperor Wu of the Han Dynasty (140 B.C.-87 B.C.), the capital granary was a large-scale warehouse used to store and exchange food. Its capacity was often enough to store tens of thousands of cubic meters of grain. Thanks to this small piece of eaves tile, the ruins of such a significant site were discovered. The ruins of the capital granary were large in scale and nicely preserved. They were the largest architectural ruins of the granary from the Western Han Dynasty ever found and are of important value for studying the history of architecture, economy, canal transportation and shipping during the Han Dynasty.

• "兰池宫当"瓦当（汉）

兰池宫在咸阳市东25里。宫内水流曲折、水域宽广，山水相依，宫阁掩映，为园林佳境。兰池宫与秦都咸阳近在咫尺，是皇家的游乐场所，秦朝末年，兰池宫遭毁弃。

Eaves Tile with Characters of Lanchi Palace (Han Dynasty, 206 B.C.-220 A.D.)

Located 12.5 km east of Xianyang City, the Lanchi Palace had a tortuous water flow, a wide and vast water area, mountains and rivers, as well as shaded platforms and pavilions. With its location so close to Xianyang, the capital of Qin, the Lanchi Palace was a resort for the amusement of the imperial families. It was destroyed at the end of the Qin Dynasty (221 B.C.-206 B.C.).

• "黄山"瓦当拓片

陕西兴平境内出土,直径15厘米。篆书"黄山"二字,字体柔美,安排布局尽显线条之美,肃穆中有古朴厚重之气。黄山宫,建于西汉惠帝二年(前193年),是西汉上林苑内重要的狩猎区。

Rubbings of Eaves Tile of Mount Huang

Excavated in Xingping, Shaanxi Province, this eaves tile has a surface of 15 cm in diameter. The characters of Mount Huang (黄山 in Chinese) were written in seal script with tender and soft line strokes beautifully arranged, showing a sense of solemnity and simplicity. Built in the second year of Emperor Hui of the Western Han Dynasty (193 B.C.), the Palace of Mount Huang was an important hunting area in the Shanglin Garden during the Western Han Dynasty (206 B.C.-25 A.D.).

• "万岁"瓦当(汉)

在吉语文字瓦当中,"千秋万岁"系列瓦当所占数量最多,流行时间最长,分布范围最广。"千秋万岁""万岁""千秋""富贵万岁"等文字的意思都是岁月长久。

Eaves Tile with Characters of Longevity (Han Dynasty, 206 B.C.-220 A.D.)

Among those eaves tiles with auspicious texts, the longevity series make up the most. They were popular for the longest time and enjoyed the widest distribution. The meanings behind such texts as longevity forever, longevity, 1,000 centuries and wealth for 1,000 centuries all related to everlasting.

- "羽阳千岁"瓦当（汉）

  羽阳宫建于秦孝公时期，汉代修缮后继续使用。从该瓦形制和字体来看为汉羽阳宫的瓦当。

  Eaves Tile with Characters of Long Live of Yuyang Palace (Han Dynasty, 206 B.C.-220 A.D.)

  The Yuyang Palace was built during the reign of Duke Xiao of the Qin State. It was repaired and used during the Han Dynasty. Based on its shape and the characters on it, it belonged to the Yuyang Palace during the Han Dynasty.

- "延年益寿"瓦当（汉）

  用"延年益寿"等吉祥语句做纹饰的瓦当寓意长生祥和。

  Eaves Tile with Characters of Longevity and Prolonged Life (Han Dynasty, 206 B.C.-220 A.D.)

  The text of Longevity and Prolonged Life used on the inscription-patterned eaves tiles serves to express the auspicious meanings of long life and harmony.

- **"长乐未央"瓦当（汉）**

  西汉的宫殿以"长乐"为宫名，体现了帝王"君与臣民常和"的美好愿望；"未央"的意思是未尽，没有穷尽，是希望汉代传之"千秋万岁"。但此瓦当并不只是长乐宫和未央宫专用瓦当，"长乐未央"是中国古人的泛用吉语。考古挖掘出土的这种瓦当有很多种，一般都为圆形，中间为乳丁，用单线或双线十字分割，上书"长乐未央"四个字，字体都处于篆隶之间，具有鲜明的时代特征。

  Eaves Tile with Characters of *Changle Weiyang* (Han Dynasty, 206 B.C.-220 A.D.)

  A palace was named *Changle* in the Western Han Dynasty (206 B.C.-25A.D.) to signify the beautiful wishes that the emporor and his subjects hold a relationship in harmony and happiness. Another palace named *Weiyang*, meaning limitless and unending, is meant to indicate that the Han Dynasty will last for 1,000 centuries. However, this eaves tile was not specifically used in the Changle Palace or Weiyang Palace. *Changle Weiyang* was a generic phrase for auspicious significance in ancient China. A lot of such eaves tiles have been excavated. Most of them are cylindrical in shape, with a stud pattern in the middle, divided by a cross in single or double lines into quarters where each of the four characters *Chang*, *Le*, *Wei* and *Yang* are written. The characters are in between the seal script and the clerical script, which offer distinctive characteristics of the time.

- **"亿年无疆"瓦当（汉）**

  "亿年无疆"瓦当是文字瓦当中的名品，多出土于汉长安城（今陕西西安）遗址。

  Eaves Tile with Characters of Limitless Billions of Years (Han Dynasty, 206 B.C.-220 A.D.)

  The eaves tile of Limitless Billion of Years is a famous item among all the inscription-patterned eaves tiles. Most of them were unearthed from Chang'an City (currently Xi'an in Shaanxi Province) during the Han Dynasty (206 B.C.-220A.D.).

- **"永奉无疆"瓦当（汉）**

此瓦当出土于陕西咸阳，为西汉皇室宗庙用瓦。瓦当字体为当时流行的小篆体，笔画非常纤细。整个瓦当古朴大气。

Eaves Tile with Characters of Unending Support (Han Dynasty, 206 B.C.-220 A.D.)

Most of these eaves tiles were excavated from Xianyang in Shaanxi Province and had been used for the imperial ancestral temples during the Western Han Dynasty (206 B.C.-25A.D.). The characters on the eaves tile are written in the small seal script, a popular script at that time, with very slim strokes. The entire eaves tile conveys a quaint and ancient atmosphere with a hint of dignity and calmness.

- **"飞鸿延年"瓦当（汉）**

一只鸿雁双翅展开，首尾两翼呈十字形，颈部伸得又长又直，这是鸿雁高飞时的典型动作。"延年"二字刻在双翅之上，似被鸿雁托起，有明显的汉隶风格。这是祭祀日月山川的神殿所使用的瓦当，流行于西汉中期，属吉语瓦当，表现出人们对美好生活的向往，对延年益寿的渴望。与"飞鸿延年"瓦当同时代的还有刻着"延寿长久"以及"延寿长相思"等字样的瓦当。

Eaves Tile with Characters of Prolong Life on a Swan Goose (Han Dynasty, 206 B.C.-220 A.D.)

A swan goose is portrayed with both wings spread out and its neck stretched long and straight. Its spread-out wings and the head and tail form a cross shape. It is a typical action for swan geese when they are flying high. Each of the two characters for Prolonged Life (延年 in Chinese), apparently in the clerical script of the Han Dynasty, was carved on the wings as if they were held up by the swan goose. Used in the halls for worshiping the sun, moon, mountains and rivers, this eaves tile was very popular during the mid-Western Han Dynasty and belongs to the eaves tiles with auspicious words to express people's desire for a better life as well as longevity. There are also similar tiles with such characters as prolonged life forever and long missing for prolonged life contemporary to the eaves tile of Prolong Life on a Swan Goose.

• "维天降灵延元万年天下康宁"瓦当（汉）

此瓦又称"十二字瓦"，在咸阳、西安的汉代长安城遗址均有出土。直径16—17厘米，瓦面上、下、左、右各有一草叶纹，文字与花纹间隙处填以乳钉纹。当面篆书，作三竖行布字，每行四字，右读为"维天降灵，延元万年，天下康宁"。统治者以自然现象附会神灵祥瑞之兆，又取警示之意，以期王朝永固。

Eaves Tile with Characters of Heavenly Blessed Longevity and Peace (Han Dynasty, 206 B.C.-220 A.D.)

Also known as the Twelve-character Eaves Tiles, these tiles were unearthed in the ruins of Chang'an City from the Han Dynasty in the locations of Xianyang and Xi'an. The tile is 16 to 17 cm in diameter and each of its surfaces on the top, bottom, left and right contains a grass pattern. The space between the characters and the patterns was filled in with the patterns of studs. Written in the seal script, with 4 characters vertically lined up in 3 columns, the text is meant to be read horizontally from right to left with the literal meaning that a ruler is bestowed with good spiritual omens in natural phenomena to maintain a peaceful world. It also meant a type of warning to keep the dynasty strong and everlasting.

• "永受嘉福"瓦当（汉）

此件瓦当的"永受嘉福"四字为虫鸟篆，体式优美，结构匀称，线条流畅。

Eaves Tile with Characters of Forever with Good Fortune (Han Dynasty, 206 B.C.-220 A.D.)

The four characters Forever with Good Fortune (永受嘉福 in Chinese) on this eaves tile were written in the bird-and-insect seal script, beautiful in style, balanced in structure and fluent in flowing lines.

"仁义自成"瓦当（汉）

从汉武帝开始，儒学成为中国传统文化的主导思想。"仁义自成"，意为人只要有了"仁义"，一切事情都会取得成功。

Eaves Tile with Characters of Everything from Kindness and Righteousness (Han Dynasty, 206 B.C.-220 A.D.)

Since the reign of Emperor Wu of the Han Dynasty, Confucianism had become the dominant ideology in Chinese culture. The text Everything from Kindness and Righteousness means that as long as a person possesses a sense of kindness and righteousness, he will be successful in everything.

"汉并天下"瓦当（汉）

此瓦当出土于汉代长安城内建章宫遗址。西汉初年，汉武帝派卫青、霍去病连续三次大规模北伐匈奴，汉朝北方威胁解除。同时，汉朝加强了中原与西域的联系，可谓天下归一。

Eaves Tile with Characters of the Unification of the Han Dynasty (Han Dynasty, 206 B.C.-220 A.D.)

Unearthed mostly from the ruins of Jianzhang Palace in Chang'an City of the Han Dynasty, the theme of this eaves tile is related to Emperor Wu's success in putting down the invasion of the Huns. During the early years of the Western Han Dynasty, Emperor Wu dispatched General Wei Qing and General Huo Qubing to launch three consecutive massive northern expeditions against the Huns. The Huns were eventually defeated and the threat to the Han Dynasty from the north was lifted. Meanwhile, the Han Dynasty also strengthened the relationship between the central plains and the western regions, which could be seen as the unification of the Han Dynasty.

• "官"字瓦当(汉)
Eaves Tile with the Character of *Guan* (Official) (Han Dynasty, 206 B.C.-220 A.D.)

秦砖汉瓦
Qin Bricks and Han Tiles

• "与华相宜"瓦当（汉）
Eaves Tile with Characters of *Yuhua Xiangyi* (Han Dynasty, 206 B.C.-220 A.D.)

- "千秋万岁与天无极"瓦当（汉）
Eaves Tile with Characters of Living Forever (Han Dynasty, 206 B.C.-220 A.D.)

- "悲哉冢当"瓦当（汉）
Eaves Tile of a Tomb (Han Dynasty, 206 B.C.-220 A.D.)

• "关"字瓦当（西汉）

（图片提供：FOTOE）

Eaves Tile with Character of *Guan* (Strategic Pass) (Western Han Dynasty, 206 B.C.-25 A.D.)

• 瓦当砚（清）

很多瓦当被文人墨客制成瓦当砚台（砚台是专用于磨墨的器具，与笔、墨、纸合称"文房四宝"，是中国书法的必备用具），带进了书斋，与中国书法结下不解之缘。

Eaves Tile Inkstone (Qing Dynasty, 1616-1911)

Many eaves tiles were converted into inkstones by scholars and literati (The inkstone is an item specifically used for grinding ink. It is one of the Four Treasures of the Study in Chinese tradition, together with the brush, ink and paper). An inkstone is a necessary item in Chinese calligraphy and introduced into the study room, forging an indissoluble bond with Chinese calligraphy.